Feedback

“This volume is one of the more recent on the topic since the discovery in the 1990s. It commends itself for being a shorter volume and still providing a solid amount of detail. The photos are nicely presented and the chapters well marked out. The descriptions of the technologies and science used for this amazing find are explained well and the biographical information as to the team members is thorough.” Amazon Verified Paperback Purchase -

“Yes the Ötzi book was very good. Now I'm no historian or expert on archeology but it’s good to see RV put to use in such manner and with excellent results. I just hope the archeology and historical community find it of some use. What have you done to spread the knowledge in this book to these guys?”

“This version of how Ötzi died is clearly more plausible than the Museum's Neolithic arrow shot conclusion. This book is loaded with pictures that make the case for why Otzi was at 10,500 feet, where he came from and where he was headed. It will most probably change the nature of the discussion.”

From the Museum: “We are actually organizing a special exhibition on the 20th anniversary of the Iceman’s found. (finding) The exhibit will start in March 2011 and end on January. We would like to show the drawing of Ötzi among other reproductions of Ötzi (how he may have looked). How can we obtain the rights to show this drawing to our visitors? Of course we will mention the author/ owner of the copyright as written in the book.”
South Tyrol Museum of Archaeology / Südtiroler Archäologie-museum / Museo Archeologico dell’ Alto Adige, Bolzano, Italy - Ötzi’s resting place.

“I found the sketches and description of how Ötzi died very revealing and once again show cases just how good Joe is as a world class remote viewer.”

“I do find your book very interesting and trust that future discourse can spawn a better understanding of "the Man in The Ice". I would be interested in future cooperation in the field of Ötziology.”

"I have finally had a chance to sit down and give Ötzi the Iceman a fair and thorough reading. In the last decade, there has been a tremendous amount of research on Ötzi's corpse, almost all in English but in scholarly journals that are sometimes difficult to find. Many thanks for calling this novel perspective on Ötzi to my attention, but unfortunately, I'm not able to reconcile the para-psychological approach with my own belief in the primacy of empirical analysis. Good luck in continuing to try to validate the remote viewing perspective through challenging it with empirical evidence!"
With kind regards, Peter Bogucki
Archaeologist and Associate Professor
Princeton University - Princeton, New Jersey, USA

"Great graphics! Our best ideas come when we have to defend our biased views. Thanks for the challenge. We can always agree to disagree without being disagreeable. You have the advantage of having McMoneagle on your side."

"Having been part of a group in the mid 1980's that worked to solve cold-case murders using psychometry, the Army's RV program certainly was exciting to consider, when I heard about it."

"I had just finished reading the book Evidential Details which you co-authored with Mr. McMoneagle. I have much respect for Mr. McMoneagle's "insights" by means of "Remote Viewing.'"

"I liked this story the best of any of them. The color photos of the mountains are beautiful. Not too much science. Seems very logical that he... (details inside) ...and his equipment spread out as it did."

"If people realized that because remote viewing is real, it changes the way we must understand everything else, they'd all be reading your books... but instead they are in watching American Idol :-). I hope you continue to produce even more in this series of books."

"Mr. McMoneagle prognosticated the Princess D. event very well. My plaudits! It provides very nice credentials."

"Please give details how to get a signed copy."

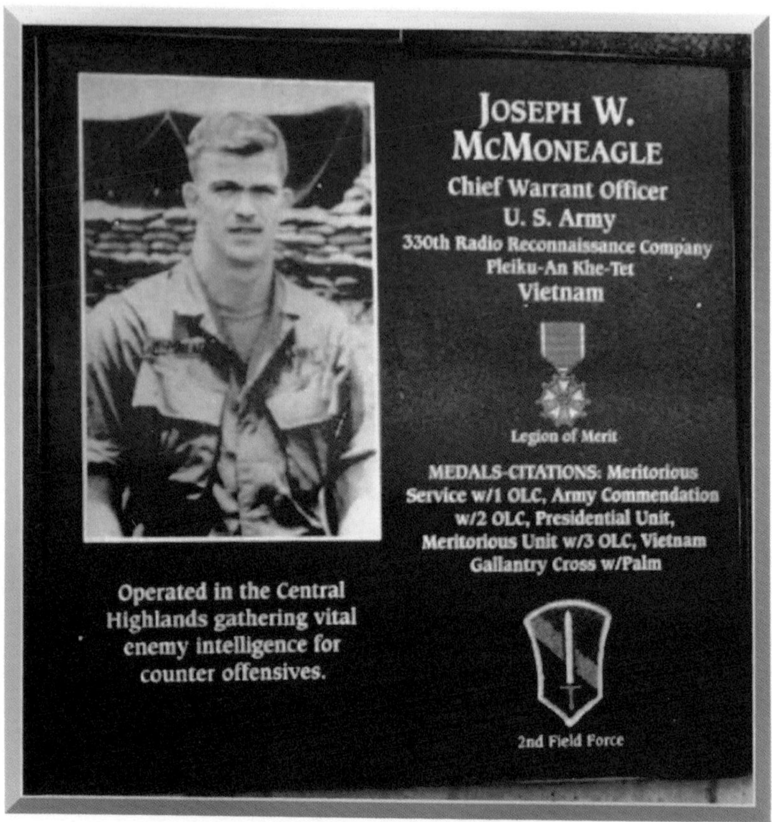

The Bronze Plaque on the Honorary Wall

In what is clearly the most fascinating component of U.S. Military History, Joseph McMoneagle is the only man to be awarded multiple medals for consistent accuracy in Controlled Remote Viewing (psy-functioning) by any military. As *Operation Star Gate's* Number One Military Intelligence asset at Fort Meade, Maryland, he was the Pentagon's go to man when data could not be obtained by any other means or was time sensitive.

Medals Received

Legion of Merit

Meritorious Service

Citations

Meritorious Service with **one** Oak Leaf Cluster;[1]
Army Commendation with **two** Oak Leaf Clusters, Presidential Unit;
Meritorious Unit with **three** Oak Leaf Clusters;
Vietnam Gallantry Cross with Palm for gathering enemy intelligence for Allied counter offensives.

The Quick Take

"Authority to award the Legion of Merit Medal is reserved for general officers and flag (Naval) officers in pay grade O-9 (e.g. Lieutenant General and Vice Admiral) and above..." - *Wikipedia.org.*

Based on the quality of the Intelligence data, the Military's Decorations Committee selected the medal with the following prerequisites:

The U.S. Army's *Legion of Merit* Medal Bestowal Requirements

The award is given for service rendered in a clearly exceptional manner. For service not related to actual war the term "key individual" applies to a narrower range of positions than in time of war and requires evidence of significant achievement. In peacetime, service should be in the nature of a special requirement or of an extremely difficult duty performed in an unprecedented and clearly exceptional manner.

Once it was confirmed what this soldier could do, these Services submitted targets:

During his career, Mr. McMoneagle has provided ...informational support to the Central Intelligence Agency (CIA), *Defense Intelligence Agency* (DIA), *National Security Agency* (NSA), *Drug Enforcement Agency* (DEA), *Secret Service, Federal Bureau of Investigation* (FBI), *United States Customs* (ICE),*the National Security Council (*NSC), *most major commands* (Army, Navy, Air Force, Intelligence) *within the Department of Defense* (DOD), *and hundreds of other individuals, companies, and corporations.*

Paragraph from Mr. McMoneagle's CV.

The Evidential Details Mystery Series

Decorated United States Military Intelligence Psychic Remote Viewer solves some of History's Greatest Mysteries

U.S. Army Legion of Merit Medal

Ötzi the Iceman

Seeds/McMoneagle

2021
The Logistics News Network, LLC. Chicago, Illinois

The Evidential Details Mysteries Series

Otzi the Iceman includes biographical references.

The Evidential Details
Imprint, a Division of
Logistics News Network, LLC.

Archeology – European History - Neolithic People – Ötzi the Iceman - Ötzal Alps – Langtaufers Valley – Bio-archeology – Paleolinguistics – Paleo-ethnological – Paleozoological – Paleoecological – Paleobotanical – McMoneagle, Joseph W. – Puthoff PhD., Dr. Harold E. – Remote Viewing – Stanford Research Institute – Neurophysiology - Anomalous Cognition

ISBN: 978-0-9826928-1–3
Library of Congress Card Number: 2010904603

Book design by LNN.

Printed in the United States of America

If you are unable to purchase this, or our other history books in your local bookstore, visit our web site at **www.EvidentialDetails.com**

Table of Contents

Section II

Section III

Acknowledgement

We would like to acknowledge the people or corporations that helped illustrate or evaluate this book.

- Certain Doctors at the former First Health Group Corp;
- The South Tyrol Archaeology Museum, Bolzano, Italy;
- University of Austria - Innsbruck
    - Dr. Walter Leitner; Department Head, Institute for Archeology;
    - Dr. Josef Aisleitner - Professor;
- Alda Plierys – Registered Nurse in the Chicago, IL. area;.
- The people at Alpenwelt Verlag, GMBH.

“The Iceman now lies in a specially built chamber at the South Tyrol Museum of Archaeology in Bolzano, Italy, that keeps him at –6 degrees Celsius (43°F) and roughly 99 percent humidity.”

Preface

In the United States Ötzi the Iceman does not get the public recognition he deserves. That is because, as Europe's archeological "show of the 20th century", it is about heritage. The language is notated in German and Italian, and points of interest are foreign to English speakers. So, double naming, untranslated research works, foreign language web sites, non-scientific language translation engines, and the ever present need to convert everything out of metric for American readers, slowed research. The general rule was that German vs. Italian names were selected by English syllabolic efficiencies.

Of all the books in the *Evidential Details Mystery Series*, this was the most challenging in its efforts to satisfy public and academic interests. The Bioarcheology, Paleo-ethnological, Paleo-zoological, Paleo-ecological, Paleo-botanical, sciences, with the attendant medical terminology, may be important to some. But the masses simply want to know what happened to Ötzi. Nonetheless, we considered that the academic language universe would be a key component to acceptance.

Ötzi's trail to the Similaun involved less conjecture than was anticipated. What ancient mountain trails were available became the research. Once it was known where he lived, his mindset and that he headed east, you realize there was only one passageway. There may be tweaks to this scenario, revisions in hiking times, etc. But, at least we now know where to start and why he died on the eighth day of his journey.

All in all this was a wonderful target to work. To date this is the only effort that unifies Ötzi's various death theories into a simple understandable package that is fully plausible. We hope you will find a new appreciation of Archaeology and Anthropology in our Evidential Details *Ötzi the Iceman*.

Conceptual Nomenclature

"The worst term of all is 'psychic'. No stable definition has ever been established for it, and there are great hazards in attempting to utilize a term which has not much in the way of an agreed-upon definition.

Supporters do assume that it refers to extraordinary, non-normal (paranormal) activities of mind. But skeptics assume it refers to illusion, derangement and a variety of non-normal or abnormal clinical psychopathologies."

Remote Viewing - One of the Superpowers of the Human Bio-Mind; Remote Viewing and its Conceptual Nomenclature Problems by Ingo Swann (09Jan96)

Military Targeting Follow-up

"Det G's[1] viewers looked at projects ranging from the status of a cement plant in a hostile country to the location of Soviet troops in Cuba. Important North Korean personalities were targeted, as well as underground facilities in Europe, chemical weapons in Afghanistan, the presence of electronic bugs in the new U.S. embassy in Moscow, the activities of a KGB general officer, a missing U.S. helicopter, tunnels under the Korean De-militarized Zone, and numerous buildings whose purposes were unknown to U.S. Intelligence."

"But frequently we never learned how close we had come to the truth, how helpful we had been, or even what we had been looking for in the first place. The targets were sometimes so highly classified that substantive evaluations could not be provided."

---

[1] Det G [Detachment G] was the remote viewing program's code name as it evolved from Operation 'Gondola Wish' to Operation 'Grill Flame'. These were the viewers who passed the Army's cut between December 1978 and January 1979. "The Army Chief of Staff for Intelligence, Major General Thompson, officially decreed that the program name, embodied in Det G, would be the focal point for all Army involvement in parapsychology and remote viewing." Op cit. Smith

Our

Introduction

To Remote Viewing

A Review of the terminology, history, and capabilities targeting

The Former Princess of Wales Diana Spencer's 1997 Auto Accident

(For the **cover story**, please refer to the Table of Contents)

"*When they* (University researchers) *did produce an incredibly accurate response during an experiment, it was in even a moderate sense "unnerving." In a greater sense, it was "earth shattering." As* (Stanford PhD) *Russell* (Targ) *implied, for some it was even "terrifying". In no case, was it ever taken lightly, as it always had a tendency to alter one's perspective towards reality and/or our place within it.*"

~ Medals Recipient Joseph W. McMoneagle~

Evidential Details

It was the peak of the Twentieth Century's Cold War 1945-1990]. The United States, the old Soviet Union, and the People's Republic of China were striving to find new ways to get an intelligence edge. During the years 1968 to 1972, the United States obtained reports that scientists in the Soviet Union had had some success with a telekinesis program that introduced atrial fibulation into frog hearts causing a heart attack. Realizing the program could target key military and political leaders, and so driven by a threat assessment, the Central Intelligence Agency funded the Stanford Research Institute (SRI) think tank in Menlo Park, California to conduct an analysis about what humanity through the ages has pondered. The doctors were to determine scientifically if psy-functioning could be taught, quantified and directed using written protocols. If so, did this represent a credible threat to the people of the United States or NATO? Their highly classified "Black Ops" program lasted from early 1972 until November 1995.

Under the most extensive and stringent experimentation two PhD's could devise, the SRI, supported by other labs and the U.S. Army, developed mankind's first "psychic" protocols. "This led to greater understanding of everything from methods of evaluation, to establishing statistical standards, to how a human brain might be appropriately studied."[i] When their findings went public, many in the academic community were privately stunned.

Eventually this covert military effort focused on real world data collection. As the years of research, analysis and application moved through the 1970's and 80's, some Army brass, with wholly personal motives, would attempt to quash the program even when research costs did not affect their budget. "All the funding had been approved on a year-to-year basis, and only then based on how effective the unit was in supporting the tasking agencies. These reviews were made semi-annually at the Senate and House select subcommittee level, where the work results were reviewed within the context in which it was happening."[ii]

Fortunately, for The People, the program was given different code names and moved around various defense budgets until much of the research and development was completed. What emerged was an incredibly "robust" database - and a process - referred to as Controlled Remote Viewing [CRV].

Much of the work took place within the 902nd United States Army Intelligence Group at Fort Meade, Maryland, whose barracks have been demolished. However, from the fastidiously maintained database emerged statistically advanced practitioners; world-class viewers whose RV data was the "best in the business." Among these, one remote viewer was the first in history to be decorated with the Army's Legion of Merit and Meritorious Service Awards (with five Oak Leaf Clusters) for having made key contributions to the Intelligence community. This individual was tasked to unlock the mysteries in this Evidential Details Book Series.

Obviously, accuracy is the name of the game. As with any horizon application process, purposefully moving the human brain into a sub-quark quantum mechanics level required new clinical terminology. As the CRV process was tested, protocols written and cautiously modified, scientists documented mental hazards to accuracy. These hindrances were cataloged and their characteristics differentiated. Year after year laboratory research determined accurate mental representations could be inhibited in a variety of ways. Some of these mental distracters included:

Physical Inclemency - Knowledge of an expected disruption like a phone call or someone about to arrive during a remote viewing session.

Advanced Visuals - A fleeting thought you cannot get rid of before a session.

Emotional Distracters or Attractors - An image you do or do not want to view regardless of the tasking.

Front Loading - Knowledge of what the target is before the viewing session. If localized, it can be used in targeting a feature within the whole picture, perhaps a house in a meadow in front of a mountain. However, without neutral wording like "The target is man-made" the object is generally rendered unworkable.

Analytic Overlay [AOL] - If a viewer is not informed about the target and not front-loaded but still has personal information about it, that knowledge may pollute the information stream rendering the session unworkable. Analytic Overlay can be a problem for any viewer. According to the military's former #1 remote viewer:

Joseph McMoneagle - Analytic overlay - CRV [Controlled Remote Viewing]**, as a format or method for learning remote viewing, offers a structure within which you can discard or identify specific elements within a session for which you are certain or not certain. Analytic Over-Lay (AOL) being a common label for something that falls within the "uncertain"**

category. However, when studied (under laboratory conditions), there is evidence that fifty percent of the time, information labeled as AOL actuality, wasn't.

I have observed just as many times, someone being smacked up against the side of the head while attempting CRV because they had strayed from the given format and slipped into AOL. I think that sometimes you may forget that CRV was developed within the hallowed halls of SRI and was taught there for years. I saw very little difference in the AOL pitfalls with CRV and other methodologies. I did see that to some extent it was a highly polished technique, which was more easily transferred through training.

With this quick overview of the subconscious transference of recollections, we turn to the remote viewing of the Princess Diana Spencer's accident in the early morning hours of August 31, 1997. As this researcher found, how one targets is critical to the result. In the fall of 1997, the massive press coverage of Princess Diana's accident and funeral emerged as a very real overlay problem. There had been much less news coverage at the hotel, so the Hotel Ritz in Paris, France, rather than the crash site, was targeted. At the time, this event was less than two months old. No accident report had been completed. Upon request, an envelope, with a second target envelope inside, was mailed to Joseph McMoneagle's home with nothing more than targeting coordinates and a date. A skeptical *Life Magazine* reporter was also on hand.

The viewing event started at 11:49 am on October 29, 1997. What makes these sessions interesting is that the reader can sense the Intelligence intellect. Having viewed 1200 targets in just the last two years of the military's Operation Star Gate alone, McMoneagle was the only viewer to participate in the program for twenty-three years. **Target Envelope No. 102997 - (no additional information other than what's sealed within the envelope.)**

* * *

As her size nine shoes hit the airport tarmac the former Princess of Wales Diana Spencer, 36, knew she was entitled to an escort by that special branch of the French Interior Ministry charged with guarding visiting dignitaries - the Service de Protection des Hautes Personalities (SPHP). But there would be no need of the service. This was to be a private visit.

Diana was returning from a Mediterranean yachting vacation off Northeast Sardinia. She and Emad "Dodi" Al-Fayed, [1955-1997] had been aboard the Fayed family's $27 million dollar (US$44.5m/2020), 195 foot yacht *Jonikal,* with 16 crewmembers.

At this point, "...in her relationship with Dodi Fayed she was displaying a new facet. In some ways a late developer, she had grown up and was simply having some adult fun."[iii] But the couple had been stalked by high-speed paparazzi boats wherever they went. On their last afternoon, they came ashore at the Cala de Volpe in Sardinia and the, "Paparazzi swarmed around them like bees, flashing away."[iv] Forced back to the boat, "Things came to a head when a scuffle broke out between three paparazzi and several members of the *Jonikal*'s crew."[v]

At about the same time, hundreds of miles away, a 73 year-old grandfather, Edward Williams, entered the police station in Mountain Ash, Mid Glamorgan, Wales. He reported that he had had a premonition that Princess Diana was going to die. The police log, time stamped 14:12 hours on August 27, 1997, stated:

"*He* [Williams] *said he was a psychic and predicted that Princess Diana was going to die. In previous years he has predicted that the Pope and Ronald Reagan were going to be the victims of assassination. On both occasions he was proven to be correct. Mr. Williams appeared to be quite normal.*"[vi]

Based on his previous record the police passed this report along to the department's Special Branch Investigative Unit.

Fed up with the non-stop press hassle, on Saturday August 30, Dodi and Diana boarded the Fayed's Gulfstream IV jet at Olbia airport in Sardinia and flew north. They arrived at Le Bourget Airport about 10 miles north of Paris, France at 3:20 p.m. Fayed's butler Rene Delorm recalled, "Unfortunately, we had a welcoming committee of about ten paparazzi waiting for us."[vii] About 600 feet (183 meters) away was a Mercedes and a Range Rover. "We had all seen the paparazzi, so we moved quickly. We wanted to get out of the plane and into the cars as fast as possible. (Body Guard) Trevor (Rees-Jones) was the first out of the jet..."[viii]

The entourage had a police escort from the airport up to France's highway A-1 leading to Paris. But as they entered the expressway, reporter's cars and two man motorcycle teams immediately dogged the entourage. The paparazzi were armed with powerful, maximum strength, flashes to penetrate deep into the car. Philippe Dourneau, 35, was Dodi's chauffeur. But in the Range Rover vehicle there had been an unexplained switch. At the wheel was the Assistant Chief of Hotel Security Henri Paul. It is unclear why Paul was chauffeuring that afternoon and not at the Ritz Hotel as acting Security Chief.

Once on the highway, Dodi instructed Ritz Hotel driver Dourneau to pick up speed in an attempt to elude photographers. What ensued was a high-speed pursuit with motorcycle cameramen weaving in and out shooting pictures. The motorcycle whirl was so intense Diana reportedly cried out in alarm that someone could get killed.[ix]

The photographer's strategy was to slow the convoy down. "Then a black car sped ahead of us and ducked in front of the Mercedes, braking and making us slow down so the paparazzi on motorcycles could get more pictures. They were risking their lives and ours, just to get a shot of Dodi and Diana riding in a car. "*Unbelievable*", exclaimed butler Rene Delorm.[x]

Dodi was not accustomed to this and after their high seas harassment, his patience was running thin. Pursuing for miles, the paparazzi then used phones to notify photographers ahead to form another gauntlet on the next highway segment. The Fayed cars split up in an attempt to divide the photographers. Some pursued Henri Paul as he drove to Dodi's apartment to deliver the luggage.

Finally, their Mercedes made it to Bois de Boulogne on the outskirts of Paris to visit the Fayed's Windsor Villa. They arrived about 3:45 p.m. Then they were off to the Ritz Hotel in downtown Paris at 4:35. Alerted by the cameramen the hotel entrance was by now packed with photographers which in turn generated curiosity seekers in the general public.

Once inside the hotel, Diana checked into the second floor Imperial Suite and went to have her hair done. She also made some phone calls. After the accident, London's *Daily Mail* correspondent Richard Kay stated that Diana had called him saying she was going to complete her contractual obligations through November and then go into private life.

Another call was made to psychic Rita Rogers whom Diana had been in contact with since 1994. Just three weeks earlier, on August 12, Dodi and Di had visited Rogers for a reading on Dodi.

She warned him not to go driving in Paris. "*I saw a tunnel, motorcycles, there was this tremendous sense of speed.*"[xi] Uneasy, Rogers reminded Diana about her readout concerning a Parisian tunnel saying, "*...remember what I told Dodi.*"[xii]

At seven o'clock, they left the hotel for Dodi's apartment at Rue 1 Arsene-Houssaye arriving at 7:15 p.m. Here the couple found the street so crowded they could not even open the car door. "The paparazzi literally mobbed the couple," said (32 year old former Royal Marine Kes) Wingfield. "They really disturbed and frightened the Princess, even though she was used to this. These paparazzi were shouting, which made them even more frightening. I had to push them back physically.'"[xiii] Butler Rene recalled:

"*...I could see they were being mobbed. I heard the shouting, saw the flashes going off and watched a security guard shove one of the photographers. Dodi did his best to shield Diana as Trevor and Kes fought to clear a path to the door... The princess was ashen and trembling, and Dodi was angry as they stalked through the apartment door...*"[xiv]

This was the way it was going to be. Rumors were rife about a marriage proposal and some wealthy publishers made it clear big money was available to the photographer that got the "million dollar shot". But no million dollars had been budgeted.

Later, things settled down, and Dodi had returned from shopping for two rings at the Repossi Jewelry Boutique, Rene recounted, "I met Dodi as he walked through the kitchen doorway, his eyes gleaming with excitement. It was then that he showed me the ring. *'Make sure we have champagne on ice when we come back from dinner,'* he told me urgently. *'I'm going to propose to her tonight!'*"[xv] Elated, he also phoned this proposal news to his cousin Hassan Yassin that evening.[xvi] [2]

Dodi had the Hotel staff book a 9:45 p.m. dinner reservetion at the fashionable restaurant Chez Benoit on the Rue Saint Martin. He also phoned the Ritz staff he would not be returning. As a result, Henri Paul departed for the weekend at 7:05p.m.

At 9:30 p.m., Dodi and Diana left the apartment for dinner but could not get through the crowd at the restaurant entrance. It was clear they could not enter a restaurant together. The enormous number of paparazzi forced Dodi to cancel their

---

[2] Dodi received a US$100,000/month ($164.915/2020) allowance from his father.

arrangements. The Press was controlling his special night with this special lady. A frustrated Dodi decided they should make the four mile drive to the Hotel Ritz where they could dine in France's only "safe" restaurant. But Henri Paul had gone for the weekend and the abrupt change in plans left the hotel staff with no time to prepare for their arrival.

When they arrived at the Ritz, another press riot broke out. It took Diana two whole minutes to negotiate the camera gauntlet the 20 feet from the front door drive-up to the hotel turnstile. The security camera time stamped her entrance at 9:53 p.m. Security man Wingfield said:

"*I had to protect her physically from the paparazzi, who were coming really too close to her*[.] *Their cameras were right next to her face.*"[xvii]

Furious, Dodi started shouting at his employees about no security to shield the 10-second walk up from the driveway. Shaken, the press savvy Diana wept in the lobby. Everyone was upset. With the owner's son angry, and the security force completely embattled, a decision was made to call the Security Chief back to work. Francois Tendil called Henri Paul's cell phone at 9:55 p.m.

Once safely in their room, Dodi called his father Mohammed Al-Fayed at approximately 10:00 p.m. He said the two would announce their engagement the next week when Diana returned from England.[xviii] "Diana always had the children for the last few days before they went back to school at the start of a new term, so that she could get everything ready and make sure they had the right kit."[xix] On Friday, she had called to confirm her boys would be at the airport to meet her on Sunday morning.

Dinner was ordered from the hotel's Imperial Suite restaurant. Diana's last meal was scrambled eggs with mushrooms and asparagus, then vegetable tempura with fillet of sole. As Di and Dodi were trying to dine normally, Henri Paul pushed his way back into the hotel through the lurking paparazzi.

For this targeting, the Hotel Ritz Building was tasked using the proper date, time, and location coordinates. As McMoneagle looked at a double blind envelope on his dining table, he started:

McMoneagle - I find myself standing next to a man who is inside some kind of a public building. He is approximately five feet, ten inches in height, good build, good con-

dition physically. He weighs about 165 pounds, is clean shaven, light brown hair, right handed, 38-40 years of age, and is not British or American; meaning he probably has another language other than English as his native tongue. [3]

Upon his return, Henri Paul waited around the Ritz for about two hours. He allegedly had a couple drinks at the bar. The Ritz security cameras recorded his behavior, which would be used for future analysis. As Chief of Security, he was certainly aware of their placement and recording capabilities.

McMoneagle - Building interior - Where he (Paul) **is within the building is inside of a very elaborate corridor. It runs the full length of the building and has lots of gilded paint, mirrors, thick carpets, lots of flowers, and is very fancy.**

The corridor runs straight out to a front entry which is well lit and very busy (even though my sense is that it is very late at night). There is an area off to the right of this corridor which has a lot of dark paneling and dark colors with a long bar or type of counter. So, this may be the reception area of the hotel or something like that.

Where he (Paul) **is standing is where the main corridor intersects with a short corridor that runs off at a ninety degree angle to the left. It intersects with some kind of a smaller staff or receiving area; perhaps a back door to the building. It is recessed and that is where his car is parked.**

The Etoile Limousine Company manager Jean-Francis Musa, 39, provided six luxury cars to the Ritz Hotel for their exclusive use. This Mercedes was licensed as a Grande Remise auto meaning only a licensed chauffeur was authorized to drive it. Henri Paul did not have those credentials.

McMoneagle - Driver - I believe that he (Paul) **drives a cab or limo...on the side, because I associate him with a car, which is parked outside and he is thinking about this car, or it seems to occupy his thoughts for some reason. He is mostly interested with driving from point A to point B. I believe he is not alone and get a strong feeling of mixed male/female in energy; which either means his passenger will be gay, or**

---

[3] Paul was 167 lbs. and he was 41 years old. He had brown hair and was also balding. His native tongue was French. He spoke fluent English and some German.

consist of two people--a male and a female.

Limo is not a stretch limo but a short, black and formal kind of car. I get an impression of a Mercedes emblem or some kind of emblem like that,[4] **so I'm assuming it is a very expensive car, could be a Mercedes. It is formal and black with an extended foot space in the back seat. Four doors. It is very heavy and my sense is that it might be equipped for hardened tires, etc.; which leads me to believe that at least one of the passengers** [Trevor Rees-Jones, 29] **might be a bodyguard** [but] **this may be Analytic overlay caused by the excessive feelings of security surrounding this vehicle and driver.**

* * *

Information about Henri Paul's mixed motivations have come to light in the years since the accident. Born one of five brothers on July 3, 1956 in the port town of Lorient, France, he had a Bachelors Degree in Mathematics and Science from the Lycee St. Louis and had won several contests for his skill as a classical pianist. He became a pilot in 1976 but was unable to qualify as a jet fighter pilot when he joined the French Air Force in 1979. Paul did however achieve the rank of Lieutenant while assigned to Security in the French Air Force Reserves.

In 1986, Paul helped setup Ritz Security. He went on to become Assistant Director. On the day of the accident, he was carrying 12,560 francs (US$2,280/$3760/2020) and his savings account pass-book.[5] Where the money came from is unknown, but he was one of only two men in France that had access to the automobile conversations of Dodi and Di. The ability to advise the press of their plans would have been of great value.

Personal adversity. Henry Paul had recently been passed over for promotion a second time by Hotel Ritz management. The first disappointment had come on Jan 1, 1993 when the nod went to colleague Jean Hocquet even though Paul was obviously in

---

4 The Mercedes S 280 sedan, valued at about $100,000 (US$164.915/2020) was engineered with eight advanced safety systems. The car had a reinforced chassis and roof. It had energy absorbing front and rear end crumple zones with electronic traction control. It also had an electronic ESP sensing system, which monitored trajectory with wheel speed to sense cornering speeds.
5 Henri Paul's salary was US$40,000 ($65,965/2020) per year.

position as the number two security man. Now again, effective June 30, 1997, as "Deputy Chief" he became the defacto head of a twenty person security team while Ritz Management searched for another chief. Now economically vulnerable, Paul had been informed of this exactly one month before the accident.

Post mortem tests stated Paul had consumed two anti-depressants called Fluoxetine and Tiapride before the accident. Fluoxetine is the active ingredient in Prozac and together these drugs are commonly used to fight alcoholism. When alcohol is introduced, the intoxicant effect is multiplied. On September 17, a different laboratory's final report was issued. It stated that Henri Paul had been in, "*moderate chronic alcoholism for a minimum of one week.*"[xx] Once this became public, the Ritz's attorneys and Mohammed Al-Fayed found themselves on the defensive. An unlicensed employee now appeared criminally negligent in a multiple wrongful death accident while in Hotel Ritz employ. It now became negligent death vs. the Al-Fayeds.

France's intoxication limit is 0.50 grams per liter. One lab report stated Henri Paul's blood alcohol level was 1.87 g/l. This was the equivalent drinking eight or nine shots of whiskey in what was found to be an empty stomach. The Paris Prosecutor's Office Report stated:

"*On this particular point, numerous expert's reports examined following the autopsy on the body of Henri Paul rapidly showed the presence of a level of pure alcohol per litre of blood of between 1.73 and 1.75 grams, which is far superior, in all cases, than the legal level.*

Similarly, these analyses revealed as [did] *those carried out on samples of the hair and bone marrow of the deceased, that he regularly consumed Prozac and Tiapridal, both medicines which are not recommended for drivers, as they provoke a change in the ability to be vigilant, particularly when they are taken in combination with alcohol.*"[xxi]

So had Henri Paul been out drinking? He had returned to the Ritz two hours and fifty minutes after departing. But no one knew where he was or what he was doing when he received the Ritz phone call. Subsequent investigations about who had seen Paul during this period failed to provide a single witness. In Paris, in the fall of 1997, there was a real fear of liability for anyone acknowledging Paul had been drinking in their establishment.

Nonetheless, the French media reported "*someone*" saw Paul drinking "aperitifs" between 7:05 and 10:08 p.m. that evening. "Someone" is wide open. But it means that after he got the urgent call to return at 9:55 p.m., he dallied almost another quarter-hour before departing which is hard to believe given the tone of the call. This was unsatisfactory. The critical question about what Paul was doing, before returning to the hotel, remains unknown.

McMoneagle - I think he was in fact sitting in a small restaurant or coffee shop, very near where he lives. Maybe even on the corner near his house. He was alone as far as I can tell. I think he was in fact drinking coffee. I do not think he was depressed, at least not more than usual. Also, regardless of what might be said, I DID NOT get a sense that he was drunk. It is remotely possible that he was taking some kind of a medication but I doubt it.

Coffee! Not drunk! This flew in the face of the formal investigation. Months before this controversy started, we were privately aware Henri Paul was not drunk.

Henri Paul was a pilot. Research indicated it was impossible to reconcile allegations of alcoholism with Paul's recent physical examination. Unbeknownst to the authorities issuing the report, just two days before the accident, Paul had completed a "rigorous" physical examination to renew his pilot's license. His *Certificat D'Aptitude Physique et Mentale* showed, "No signs of alcoholism."[xxii] A direct medical conflict supporting McMoneagle. Is a mere statement proof Paul was drunk? Six months after these sessions, the Ritz Hotel security videos further reaffirmed our data.

Behavioral Psychologist Dr. Martin Skinner commented in Fulcrum Productions documentary for ITV. The doctor stated there were no behavioral signs of drunkenness as Henri Paul waited for Dodi and Diana.

Skinner: *I don't think there is evidence, from the video, that can suggest he looked drunk. The pictures of him walking up and down the corridor are straight and smooth. He is standing very still and there is nothing in his demeanor, from these videos, to suggest that there are any problems with his competence in this situation.*[xxiii]

Next came a statement from Trevor Rees-Jones, the front seat bodyguard sitting next to Paul. About intoxication, he said:

Rees-Jones: *I had no reason to suspect he was drunk. He did not look or sound like he had been drinking. He just seemed his normal self. He was working. He was competent. End of story. I can state quite categorically that he was not a hopeless drunk as some have tried to suggest. I like to think I have enough intelligence to see if the guy was plastered or not – and he wasn't.*[xxiv]

Neither the bodyguards, nor Dodi, or anyone else at the Hotel detected anything unusual in Paul's behavior. But there was more. Paul's blood was next reported as containing abnormally high carbon monoxide levels - twenty percent too much. How this happened has never been determined. But doctors agree it is impossible for a forty-year-old man, with that much poison in his blood stream, not to look and feel sick - too sick for high speed urban driving. When the press advanced the idea car exhaust was the source of Paul's poisoning, Dodi's father, Mohammed Al-Fayed, put the obvious question: *"How did Henri Paul get 20% carbon monoxide in his blood when my son had none?"*[xxv]

The obvious question is how you can get that much CO^2 into someone's blood stream when, due to an instantaneous death, there was no breathing, and the engine had stopped immediately.

During his last month Henri Paul had come to know what it was like to assume the Security Chief's responsibilities while the Ritz Hotel interviewed. He must have been concerned another hire may not be as accommodating as his previous colleague/boss had been. After setting up the security operation, and with a decade of service, Henri Paul now faced the possibility of being forced out by a new supervisor. Clearly, Ritz management was not taking care of Paul as a career professional.[6]

Another component of the Henri Paul enigma concerned the fact that most nations have an Embassy in Paris and many dignitaries and diplomats stay at the Ritz. Stories started to appear that Paul was in the employ of various "foreign and domestic" intelligence services. Then it was discovered he had one million francs

---

[6] The Hotel Ritz subsequently hired a former Scotland Yard Chief Superintendent John MacNamara. His background in criminal intelligence management and investigations was substantially different than Paul's Air Force Reserve security credentials.

Session Sketch

This drawing provides a rare glimpse intelligence level RV artwork. For this exercise, people and not the building were targeted. But, this sketch could be the third floor at the North Korean Embassy in Moscow, Russia, or any building, anywhere, anytime now or for a future tasking. As a person was the target, the Hotel Ritz Paris first floor was roughed out at approximately midnight on August 31, 1997. Points of interest are:

1) At the top of the page, the words **Big Bldg** appear;
2) The various circles with an **X** inside indicates where people were standing at approximately 12:15 a.m. on August 31, 1997.
3) On the left, the **Main Door** is shown with an **X** representing the Door attendant. As the hall extends to the right, the various rooms are notated.
4) Toward the bottom is a **Business** area. As you walk from the front door, **"There is an area off to the right of this corridor which has a lot of dark paneling and dark colors with a long bar or type of counter."**
5) At the top is an **Alcove** with two people inside. These individual's backgrounds – conversations – futures – mental states - deaths can be targeted at any time in the future.
6) Where the hallway comes to a junction there is a **Man**. This is Henri Paul as he monitors the activities in both corridors. What were Paul's private thoughts? **"I associate him with a car which is parked outside and he is thinking about this car, or it seems to occupy his thoughts for some reason."**
7) Behind Henri Paul is the **Laborer Area**. Next to this is the drawing date and time documenting who was where when.
8) The hallway to the **Side Door**, **"...intersects with some kind of a smaller staff or receiving area; perhaps a back door to the building. It is recessed and that is where his car is parked."** That recessed area is shown.
9) McMoneagle also shows the **Formal Black Limo**'s position by the back door and correctly identified the automobile's color and manufacturer's hood ornament (bottom right).

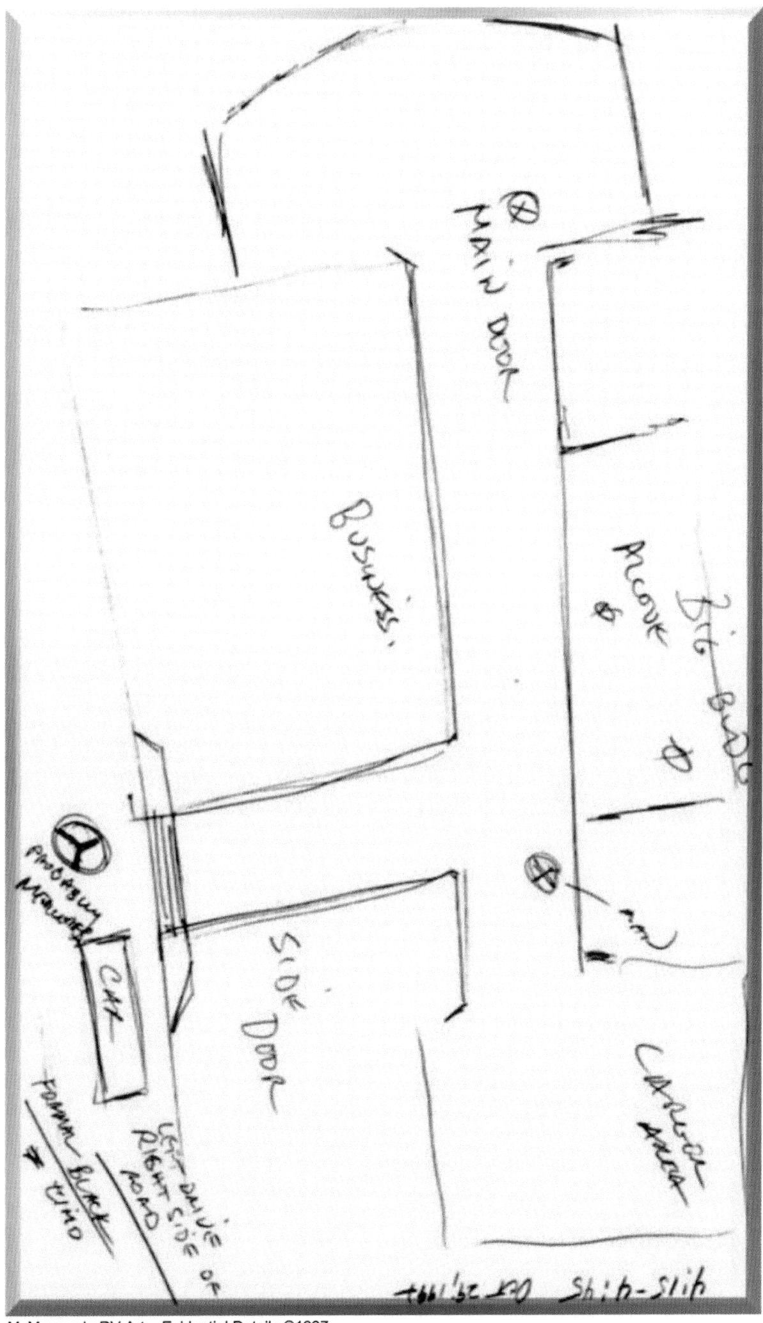

McMoneagle RV Art – Evidential Details ©1997

Hotel Ritz Paris first floor sketch with car (lower right) as viewed from Virginia.

(US$200,000–$250,000/$329,827-$412,285/2020) spread among eighteen bank accounts in an attempt to disguise the fact. Al-Fayed would later make the claim Paul had spent at least three years working for British intelligence. Where he got this information, or if it is true, is unknown. Paul was also allegedly in contact with the Direction General de la Securite Exterieure [DGSE] - French Intelligence. He probably worked for any number of paying interests or intelligence agencies on a spot basis.

So, we were left with a feigned alcoholic dead man; with employment and big money surveillance concerns; ordered to violate multiple traffic laws; by a romantically aggravated boss in love with the world's foremost attractive woman.

Henri Paul was uncertain about his future. He had to have been anxious about protecting his access to the Hotel Ritz time and date stamped video-monitoring system. He must have been concerned about his ability to generate big income by documenting high profile personalities, celebrities, or foreign dignitaries' arrivals and departures with anyone.

But all of a sudden, that night there was a positive side to the whole discordant affair. A rare opportunity to make a positive impression on the owner's son was at hand. In the wee hours of August 31, 1997, it would have been impossible for any driver to presume to caution a provoked Dodi Al-Fayed about safe driving on nearly deserted streets. As characterized by French Union Official Claude Luc:

> "*If one of the Fayeds gives you an order, you follow it. No questions asked.*"[xxvi]

Whatever his prospects, Security Chief Henri Paul was illegally behind the wheel again. He was laid to rest in Lorient, France on September 20, 1997. Father Léon Théraud gave the sermon at Sainte Therese Church.

* * *

On Saturday night, now Sunday morning August 31, a physically aggressive horde of stalkarazzi and other onlookers, estimated at approximately 130 people, jockeyed for position at the Hotel Ritz front turnstile. Diana Frances Spencer and her boyfriend Dodi, son of Egyptian born multi-millionaire Mohammad Al-Fayed, needed a second car to exit the hotel's back entrance. Because of the paparazzi, a front door - back door scheme had been set-up for their return to Dodi's apartment. Dodi would take Diana out the back leaving his personal Range Rover in front as a decoy.

McMoneagle – Car is parked on the right side of the road (right side driving) which would rule out England, Bahamas, Hong Kong, Japan, etc. It is night and it is dark. The time for this event is current, probably 1985 to 1997. I will try and bring that down to a shorter period later.

The tag on the limo is elongated, with letters and numbers--which is a European style of tag (License 688 LTV 75). **My sense is that there may actually be two colors of tags on this car, or that it has inter-changeable tags, which are changed, dependent upon where it is being operated. One is yellow with black lettering; the other is white with black lettering. It may be that there are two different colored tags on the car simultaneously—one color on one end, one color on the other.**

This is a superb surveillance example. The yellow license with black lettering was on the rear bumper. As it turned out, the color license designated a private car. The white tag is a "for hire" vehicle. From this the reader can gather the type of information available through remote viewing should this car have been driving a foreign dignitary.[7]

After some hallway discussion, Ritz chauffeur's Philippe Dourneau and Jean-Francois Musa drove two decoy vehicles to the hotel's front door. The night was clear. The temperature was 77 degrees [25C]. Their engines were revved up as Dodi and Diana hurried out the back door at 12:20 a.m.

Diana's last few minutes on earth were now inexorably caught-up in the emotional web of her incensed boyfriend and his driver's employment needs. Some paparazzi across the Rue Cabman observed them as Trevor, Diana, and then Dodi came through the turnstile and got into the Mercedes. Henri Paul pulled out and the chase was on.

McMoneagle - Believe the car is the main focus of this

---

[7] In Foreign Relations, these plates could indicate a restricted territory vehicle. If unauthorized, remote viewers could be tasked on who issued both types of plates to the same party. This inquiry would remain secret, while perhaps unmasking a corrupt government official, or a mole in the host country's bureaucracy.

target. The man [Paul] **may also be of interest.... I believe this target has to do with an accident that probably occurred either in the very late night hours or possibly very early morning hours. Traffic is very light and the streets are very quiet. Get a sense that there are few cars about, in a place which is usually crawling with cars.**

Associated Press

A back door security camera photograph, time stamped 12:19 a.m. just before they departed. It shows Henri Paul (left) conversing with Dodi and Diana with Trevor Rees-Jones' head in the background.

The Mercedes is moving very fast, from what apparently is a northwest...direction. Have a sense that it goes over an overpass or cloverleaf kind of interchange, which then drops straight down, into a tunnel.

The car traveled toward the Seine River's westbound express street referred to as the Cours la Reine. Then they entered the Alexander III & Invalides Tunnel Bridge. The tunnel is 330 meters (361 yards) long.

McMoneagle - It [Mercedes] **then exits the tunnel and covers a large curve of open road, which enters another tunnel like area, only this second tunnel is not enclosed completely. Have a sense of concrete tiers on one side... Vehicle is moving very quickly, perhaps in the neighborhood of approximately 100 MPH** [162 km/h]**, maybe even a bit faster (in some spurts or straightaways).**

The curve in the road is 480 meters [.3 miles] in front of the next tunnel, which provides an acceleration area. But with a subsequent curve and dip, it was not possible to negotiate that section of highway at high speed.

McMoneagle - In my opinion, the driver was driving way beyond the speeds that would have been comfortable for the place and time. I believe he was well trained as a driver but not for the place or speed at which he was driving. I have a sense the driver was doing his damnedest to carry out the instructions of those he was carrying, but was operating at speeds and conditions that even he was never really trained to drive within. I think he was the professional here and was being egged on by the passengers.

McMoneagle was correct on this detail. Paul had attended special driving courses in Stuttgart, Germany from 1988 through 1993, receiving high marks, and Dodi knew this.

These sessions took place approximately ninety days before the release of the official fifty-two page report entitled, *Accident de Passage Souterrain de l'Alma. Paris Dimanche 31 Aout 1997, Oh25. Propostition d'Analyse Scientific et Technique. Synthese et Conclusions.* French Engineer Jean Pietri had been commissioned to write an engineering crash analysis, which went on to verify this remote viewing material.

The distance from the first tunnel to the Pont de l'Alma tunnel is 1.2 kilometers (.75 mile). The speed limit is 30 mph (48km). It is here that published accounts differ. Apparently, three people witnessed four to six paparazzi motorcycles attempting to pull alongside the speeding Mercedes. Other accounts say the paparazzi were a quarter of a mile behind when the Mercedes entered the tunnel. In either event, it was all futile. Notified by telephone, reporters had already assembled at Dodi's apartment entrance, million-dollar picture in mind.

McMoneagle – The Mercedes pulls out to pass a slower moving vehicle at a point in the road where the road ahead rises upward to a secondary overpass. Because of the rise in the road, the driver can't see on-coming traffic in time to avoid it, specifically at this speed.

The final report verified this was correct. French accident investigator Jean Pietri subsequently stated:

"To our surprise, we observed that the field of view is extremely limited. Passing cars disappear from sight well before they actually enter the tunnel because the descending road is obscured by a retaining wall. To the left the field of vision is blocked by a row of trees."[xxvii]

About 40 meters (44 yards) in front of the tunnel the Mercedes hit a gap in the pavement, which further destabilized control. As the car passed a white Fiat Uno at break neck speed Henri Paul saw another car dead ahead.

McMoneagle – I believe he sees an on-coming car which appears to be some kind of a black or dark green sedan. I want to say Citreon, but I'm really not sure. Probably a smaller two door car, two passengers; get a sense of dark green or green-black combination, which could mean a green **a smaller two door car, two passengers; get a sense of dark green or green-black combination, which could mean a green** (body) **and black** (trim).[8]

Mohammad Medjahdi was driving a Citroen BX with his girlfriend Souad in the tunnel ahead of the Fiat Uno.

McMoneagle – Dodi's last words - Have a fleeting sense that he [Paul] **is being ordered to go faster and to do more erratic things, to avoid something. He** (Paul) **is essentially being ordered to do what he is doing.**

To avoid the on-coming traffic, the Mercedes driver swerves hard to the right and catches the small car he is passing [Fiat Uno] **with his rear bumper. Car that was passed was hit. As a result, the Mercedes slews around left, just misses the on-coming car, which** [it] **has just passed, and the driver then begins to over-correct his steering.**

Months after these sessions, French engineers confirmed the Mercedes did nick the Fiat Uno and over corrected to the right. Some tail light/head light debris was found. Engineers estimated that if the Mercedes was going 100 miles per hour the debris would have rolled sixteen meters (52.5 feet). That hit took place outside the tunnel and it is here the 18.9m (62ft) tire skid mark begins.[9]

---

[8] Here McMoneagle was inside looking through the Mercedes windshield. His use of "*oncoming*" describes the overtaking of cars. It does not refer to opposite direction traffic flow.

[9] The tail light pieces found in the tunnel belonged to a Fiat Uno manufactured between May 1983, and September 1989 by Seima Italiana. The white paint chips were called Bianco Corfu. When found, the car had been repainted.

McMoneagle - The Mercedes hits the side to left slews across and hits the right, then swings back to the left, where it catches what appears to be a concrete tier or pier (#13 pillar) **of some kind, concrete pilasters, or some kind of upright** (steel reinforced) **concrete dividers, which it hits nearly head on.**

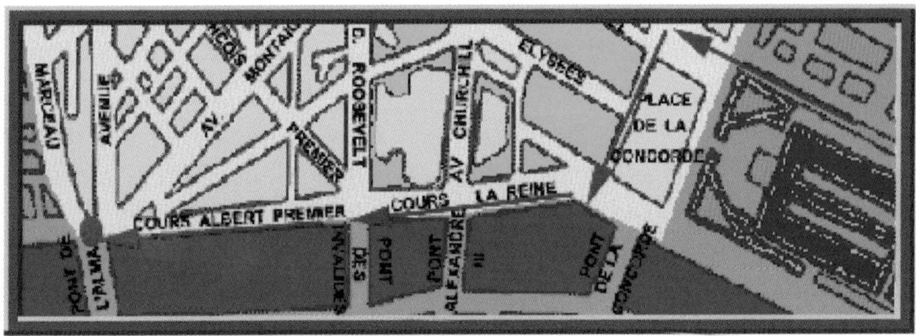

A view of their route along the Seine River. The red arrow (top right corner) points the direct route to Fayed's apartment.

At 12:24 am. There was an explosion sound in the tunnel. The subsequent engineering report confirmed Henri Paul's last evasive actions were viewed correctly. Various eyewitnesses recounted the collision. "Gaelle L., 40, a production assistant stated:

"At that moment, in the opposite lane, we saw a large car approaching at high speed. This car swerved to the left, then went back to the right and crashed into the wall with its horn blaring. I should note that in front of this car, there was another, smaller car."[xxviii]

McMoneagle - The Mercedes apparently nearly goes end over end rear to front, but doesn't quite make it [over the top]**, instead spinning twice and winds up pointing back in the direction it was coming from.**

The car spinning $1^{1/2}$ times remains unconfirmed. However, there was enough inertia for the car to have spun 540 degrees when the rear wheels were off the ground. The impact was so hard that the forward roof area was crushed down to the level of the driver's knees. This is further substantiated by the fact Diana was found facing backward in the back seat, which would not have happened with a simple 180-degree turn. N*ewsweek Magazine* reported French police estimated the car had slowed down to 85 mph at the point of impact.[xxix]

The entire trip had taken about four minutes. Trevor Rees-

Jones did not leave the hospital until October 4 - thirty-four days later. He could only recall the Fiat Uno.

Rees-Jones: "*It seems to me there was one white car with a boot which opened at the back* [hatch back], *and three doors but I don't remember anything else.*"[xxx]

Aware Henri Paul did not have alcohol in his system, we sought clarification to research about drugs in his blood stream.

McMoneagle - Substance review - I believe if the driver had drugs in his system, whatever kind they were, they were not there by his own hand. I have this sort of strange feeling that he was not deliberately drugged to hurt anyone, but maybe he was drugged to get the car stopped along the route for the "photographers" to get their shots. In other words, his control was tampered with by outside influences. I don't think he was drunk, possibly drugged, but not drunk.

Here the research came full circle. The paparazzi had attempted to slow the Hotel Ritz airport shuttle vehicles earlier that afternoon on the drive from the airport. Once it was discovered, Henri Paul had been an informant for domestic as well as foreign intelligence services we went back to McMoneagle. Could the British government have been involved?

McMoneagle - My sense is that MI-5 (British Intelligence) **did not put the stuff in his drink. However, one might contemplate that if he** [Paul] **was willing to take money from foreign intelligence operatives, he most certainly would have been open to taking money from the Paparazzi. Maybe they were hedging their bets by having a small "drink" with him in the bar before he started driving.**

And what of the high carbon dioxide levels in Dodi's blood stream? Since this viewing, there were reports of a carbon monoxide suicide in Paris that night.

McMoneagle - You have to open your perception a little bit here. He did not have to have any evidence of CO^2 in his blood for them to find CO^2 in a blood sample. You only have to switch the samples at the hospital, the morgue, or the lab. Or, pay off the guy who is doing the tests. You could also conceivably rig the test equipment. Also, there are drugs, which will give a false reading as well.

His being drugged enough to cause the accident could be attributed to a drug delivered in coffee, tea, or a drink beforehand. It could also have been sprayed on the inner edge of his door handle (driver's side), painted on the steering wheel, or inside a pair of driving gloves. He could have been shot with a needle delivery system, or pricked his hand, finger, leg, or almost any part of his anatomy on a delivery system getting into or out of the car. It can even be filmed across the pages of a book or map that he might have used to check directions on.

If he had a normal medical condition, they could have used a drug, which reacts violently with the drugs he is already taking for the medical condition. In which case they would either get false readings, or evidence of his medicinal drug, plus some other known drug which would not have been viewed as culprit in the event, simply because no one recognized the possible expected reaction. You also have problems with drugs which are binary in nature and can be delivered in two sittings, so to speak, where the victim gets part A in the morning with breakfast, part B in the evening with dinner, both of which are enzymes and when mixed... cause everything from hallucinogenic behavior, to strokes.

Now we turned to what Dodi and Diana where thinking.

McMoneagle - Back seat travelers - MAJOR PROBLEM: **When I try to access others who might have been in the car, I get heavy** [analytic] **overlay and interference as relates to Diana's death in France. My head fills up with all kinds of motorcycles, and all kinds of news... that was being broadcast about the incident. I believe there were at least two others in this target car, but digging anything out of the overlay is completely impossible.**

There is a sense from the people in the back seat that they want to be alone together, but again, I then get overwhelmed with all the Princess Diana stuff... and it all runs together. So, I can't begin to tell where [the] **overlay begins and real data ends. Would prefer to say nothing.**

It's rather interesting. I actually have not opened the envelope nor have a clue as to the real target here; but I am being overwhelmed with overlay which is self-generated. Must have been a lot of energy around the Princess Diana stuff.

Better to just go no further with it. End of Session.

An abrupt stop, on a then well-known topic, due to analytic overlay. This is a graphic demonstration of the differences between military remote viewers, storefront psychics or hot lines. The media had been saturated with Princess Diana coverage in the period between the accident and this tasking. A psychic hot-liner would have been able to talk and bill without end about what they "saw." One Operation Star Gate military remote viewer commented, "There are many "*psychics*" who have taken this type of gibberish to a finely honed skill."[xxxi] But, when McMoneagle got to the Mercedes back seat, he stopped the session. In intelligence work when you are not sure of your viewing, you must say so. Any elaboration is unethical as in life and death situations, military viewers must stay grounded in the target's realities.

Analytic Overlay [AOL] is terminology within the Controlled Remote Viewing [CRV] protocols developed by Mr. Ingo Swann for the U.S. Military Intelligence Community at the Stanford Research Institute as they developed the nomenclature. AOL can generate bad data. So, can anything be done about it?

McMoneagle - Military research - There were a number of experiments which were run to examine whether or not a remote viewer can identify "AOL" while in session. We found that it could be rarely demonstrated. Most viewers are unable to tell (accurately or consistently) when something was AOL or when it wasn't, while in session.

Facts are; Evidence produced within labs suggests that no one methodology is capable of identifying and extinguishing AOL any better than another over the long haul.

There have been significant runs of very low AOL or displays of almost no AOL which have been done by individual remote viewers. So, there are indications that some people might have a talent for producing less AOL than others. But it does not appear to be method driven since it doesn't hold up in testing across all remote viewers using the same method.

So, why should identifying AOL be important??? It is important because, while you are attempting to learn remote viewing (regardless of method), it makes you think about how and why you are "thinking" about something. It is meant to reduce the speed by which you automatically jump to a

conclusion. It also supports the structure and keeps one within it (at least until one becomes proficient enough to no longer need it.)

After the impact, eyewitnesses saw a motorcycle 30 to 40 meters behind the Mercedes slow down to observe the accident and then accelerate away from the scene. At 12:26 a.m., the Paris Fire Department - Sapeurs-Pompiers Unit - received a cell phone call from a Gaelle who was in the tunnel. Within one minute another call went out to the "service d'aid medicale urgente" (SAMU) - a civilian emergency medical service.

Inside the wreck, Diana and bodyguard Trevor Rees-Jones were still alive. One eyewitness said he heard a woman crying loudly. One of the paparazzi, Romuald Rat, indicated Diana was conscious. He claimed he told her to stay calm; that help was on the way.

Aftermath

Now pandemonium broke out as the Press fought each other to get the new million dollar shot. One photographer leaned into the car to reposition Dodi's corpse for a posed picture. Someone else came with video equipment. Within five minutes, Police Officers Lion Gagliardone and Sebastien Dorzee plowed through the crowd to the car. The police report stated:

"*I observe the occupants in the vehicle are in a very grave state. I immediately repeat the call for aid and request police reinforcements, being un-able to contain the photographers….*"[xxxii]

Officer Dorzee: "*I finally got to the vehicle... The rear passenger* (Diana) *was also alive... She seemed to be in better shape* (than Rees-Jones). *However, blood flowed from her mouth and nose. There was a deep gash on her forehead. She murmured in English, but I didn't understand what she said. Perhaps 'My God!*'[xxxiii]

Ultimately, six paparazzi were held in connection with the frenzy in the tunnel. They were arrested on suspicion of involuntary homicide and failure to assist persons in danger. Excepting the 24-year-old Romuald Rat, 40 was the average age of those arrested. Twenty film rolls were confiscated providing police with the photographic evidence they needed to confirm each man's activities that night. Three paparazzi got away.

There are no Miranda rights in France, nor is there a right to call an attorney. French authorities can hold a suspect for forty-eight hours before the prisoner must be formally charged or set free. However, it is certain Henri Paul did not have to be drunk or drugged to have had an accident at that speed.

The former Princess of Wales, Diana Spencer, arrived at the Hospital de la Pitie-Salpetriere at 2:00 a.m. She was pronounced dead at 4:00 a.m. It was then she attempted to contact her son William in Scotland. "William had had a difficult night sleep and had woken many times. That morning he had known, he said, that something awful was going to happen."[xxxiv] When he was told of his mother's death he said, "*I knew something was wrong. I kept waking up all night.*"[xxxv]

At 5:00 p.m. Prince Charles, 48, flew into Villacoublay military airfield outside Paris from Aberdeen, Scotland with Diana's sisters Sarah McCorquodale and Jane Fellows. "Diana's sisters spent most of the flight to Paris in tears. The Prince was controlled but clearly very shaken."[xxxvi] By 5:40 p.m., he was greeted at the hospital by the French President and Mrs. Jacque Chirac (1995-2007). Charles was led into a room with his two ex-sisters-in-laws where Diana lay in a coffin. He asked to be alone with the body for a moment. When he came out his eyes were red. The accident was 368 days after the finalization of their divorce.

Diana's coffin, draped in the Royal Standard's yellow and maroon, was flown home by an honor guard in a British Royal Air Force BAe146 aircraft to Northolt Air Force Base in England. She was then taken to the Chapel Royal at Saint James Place.

Undertaken by Levertons, her September 6 funeral was the largest in England since the death of former Prime Minister and Nobel Literature Prize winner Winston Churchill [1874-1965]. After the morning funeral, it was reported a million people lined the route as the body was taken from London's Westminster Abby. Different accounts estimated two to three billion people watched the day's events as the car traveled the seventy-five miles to Althorpe House. Late that afternoon her body was laid to rest on a 1,254 sq. meter (13,500 sqft) island called The Oval in a lake on the Spencer's ancestral grounds. The four hundred-year-old estate was then partially turned into a tourist attraction.

On September 9, 1997, the week after Diana was buried the Al-Fayed attorney filed civil law suits against the French periodicals *France-Dimanche* and *Paris-Match.* The complaint specified invasion of privacy with willful and wanton reckless endangerment when helicoptering "stalkerazzi" got too close over the Fayed's villa in St. Tropez. But, for the Hotel Ritz, the question became who bears responsibility for the accident? Before 1997 was out, the Fayed, Spencer, Rees-Jones and Paul families had all filed papers to be made civil parties to the investigation. Under French law, this allows them to investigate the case file and participate in any damage awards. And as for the Paparazzi's fate:

"*In accordance with articles 175, 176 and 177 of the Code of Penal Procedure; The examining magistrates find that there is no case to answer in the case of the state versus the above named* [Photographers]."[xxxvii] (Case Dismissed)

In July of 2004, after the planning, funding and construction were completed, Queen Elizabeth II personally opened the Princess of Wales Memorial Fountain in the southwest corner of London's fashionable Hyde Park.

Then, in April 2008, after a three year investigation costing $7.3 million ($12 million+/2020), a six month long British report was released which included the testimony of 278 witnesses with more than 600 exhibits generating an 832 page report stating:

"*Our conclusion is that, on the evidence available at this time, there was no conspiracy to murder any of the occupants of the car,*" Lord Stevens of Kirkwhelpington, who led the inquiry, told reporters as he presented his findings here. "*This was a tragic accident.*"[xxxviii]

In September of 2012, the French magazine Closer published paparazzi photos of Diana's eldest son's wife Kate Middleton sunbathing topless while at the Queen's nephew, Lord Linley's French chateau. A publically released statement on behalf of the Duke and Duchess said:

"*The incident is reminiscent of the worst excesses of the press and paparazzi during the life of Diana, Princess of Wales, and all the more upsetting to The Duke and Duchess for being so.*"

And as for the need to use remote viewing protocols:

McMoneagle - Pick whatever method you intend to pursue and stick to it like glue. AOL (Analytic Overlay) **is a fact of life and this will always be so. Those of you who can eventually see your way to controlling your inner-driven or more personalized prejudice while internally processing, will probably improve somewhat in reducing AOLs, but AOLs will never entirely go away.**

CRV (Controlled Remote Viewing) **is a "method" derived from a method the military used while attempting to "train" people to understand both protocol as well as what is going on in a remote viewer's head (such as processing or the lack thereof).**

I would add that formal testing in the SRI Lab showed that regardless of technique or methodology utilized, most viewers were unable to consistently identify AOLs when asked to identify them prior to feedback. I have to say most, because "a couple viewers" were able to do so during significant runs--but this is inherently talent based and not the general or common rule. I remind you all of what is termed the "AH-HA". If it were not for the Ah-ha's, there would not have been a program. At the end of the road, almost anything is right when you have finally come to understand that it is an inherent part of our nature and then you just simply can do it.

Ötzi: Wither I go, thither shall you go too;

Today will I set forth,

Tomorrow you.

Shakespeare - *Henry IV*

Otzi the Iceman

The Origin, Life and Death of

Europe's Archaeological Show of the 20th Century

We cannot properly estimate the achievements of prehistoric man, for we must guard against describing their life with imagination that transcends the evidence…

Will & Ariel Durant

Neolithic Europe, that time in history between 9,000 and 3,000 B.C. Imagine life when the Iceman's mother delivered a baby boy in a dirt hovel somewhere in northern Italy. On average her son would be only one of four children that survived to adulthood. If she lived, she must have eventually known her baby was flawed missing one row of ribs. Some scientists speculate she may have also passed on an infertility gene.

As various Alpine tribes' territories were contested, the higher technology Neoliths put the Mesoliths on the defensive. Not targeted, Ötzi's speculative boyhood location includes the Juval and Eisack Valleys as well as villages around Lake Garda and at Feldthurns. Wherever, his tribe had probably been forced out.

Sometime during Egypt's First Dynasty, Ötzi went through adolescence. This was some five hundred years before the first pyramids were constructed making masons and blacksmiths the first craftsmen. King Tutankhamen would not rule for another 1950 years; and Ramses II not for another two millennia. Ancient Rome's earliest settlements were still some 2700 years into the future. Alexander the Great would not take Babylon for another 2970 years. Jesus of Nazareth would not be born for 3,300 years. And through this period, historians estimate global population at about 100 million people.

"During these many thousands of years cities were rising in the Middle East, in Egypt, and on some of the Mediterranean islands. But in the more remote areas of Europe...prehistoric ways of living still continued."[xxxix]

As Ötzi matured, ancient British tribes were implementing Stonehenge I. Long burial mounds were under construction in France. The Irish had recently constructed astronomically sophisticated mounds along the Boyne River. In Iraq, the Sumerians were building what is considered the world's first civilization with commercial hieroglyphics. Temples were being erected in Malta, and the city of Troy and the Jericho Oasis were starting to thrive.

Uneven in its emergence, civilization was just beginning. The basis for the little documented Neolithic vs. Mesolithic displacement was cultural and resource based. The Neolithic societies formed an agricultural foundation with a multi-specie animal husbandry, meat, milk with the by-products base. These innovations sustained larger, better nourished, and longer lived populations. Whereas the pre-pottery Mesolith was a hunter-gather who needed large forested land tracts to survive.

As Alpine valley forests were steadily logged, slashed and burned, the outnumbered Mesoliths had to move on. With their furnaces, metals and comparative height and strength, the Neolith had the upper hand in any protracted conflict.

When Neolithic farming encroached, Mesolithic scouts were sent out to find a place where the hunting was good and they could live in safety. As our data was generated, most scientists believed Ötzi's final journey started from his birth camp. But, "Investigations by Wolfgang Müller of the Australian National University of the isotopic composition of the Iceman's tooth enamel suggests that he had grown up in one area but spent the last several decades of his life in a different place."[xl] Going forward, we refer to Ötzi's medical data as "Scientists" because there were a number of specialists contributing to these research reports.

Scientists: "A few faint Harris lines were detected in the proximal (nearest to the center) and distal (furthest from the center) metaphyses[10] of the tibiae.[11] Harris lines are traditionally attributed to changes in nutrition or stress during growth and development. These lines are also termed growth "arrest" or "recovery" lines to emphasize either the inciting factor in their appearance or the new bone formation necessary for their appearance."[xli] As Harris Lines and tooth enamel were not coupled together before this book's first edition, we suggest these factors illustrate the circumstances surrounding adolescent migration.

While not provable, the Baltimore Sun editorialized: "What the samples showed is that Ötzi most likely spent his childhood south of his final resting place, possibly in...the Eisack Valley. As an adult, he made his way west and lived in the Etsch Valley. In all, the evidence shows, Ötzi never strayed more than 40 miles from his childhood home."[xlii]

The combination of Ötzi's tooth enamel changes and his body's Harris Lines established:

1) Ötzi moved while he was still growing;
2) That he experienced stress during this period;
3) That malnutrition had been one of the issues.

---

[10] The growing portion of the bone.

[11] Plural for Tibia - The inner and larger leg bone between the knee and the ankle.

Where Ötzi originated remains unknown, but the move was forced upon his tribe before he became twenty, making a lasting impression on this teenager. And as the higher technology Neoliths took territorial control, Ötzi's people found themselves among the last of a dying breed.

We concluded Ötzi's tribe moved west through the Aldige River Valley. Following the valley's bend to the north, scouts led their people past a Phase One Remedello village at Lake Haidersee. Passing through, they moved into a secondary unoccupied sub-valley on the eastern side.

As the Mesoliths were being forced deeper into side valleys, "*The typical cultures of the Late Neolithic developed. But none of them crossed the passes or saddles of the main Alpine ridge. A breathing space intervened.*"[xliii] noted the Chairman of the Pre-History and Early History Department at the University of Austria, Innsbruck during this research. He was the lead South Tyrolean Iceman scientist - the late Konrad Spindler.

This transition is something of which modern man has very limited knowledge. Ötzi may be histories only example of what happened as this "breathing space" ended. Further, there is a reason his blood type K1ö DNA (the world's oldest) cannot be (exactly) matched with modern man.[xliv]

In science, where data deficiencies exist, controlled remote viewing has been quietly in use. In this instance, decorated U.S. Military Intelligence Remote Viewer Joseph McMoneagle was targeted on Ötzi's mummy in Bolzano, Italy. The targeting questions were based on the scientific community's knowledge in 1998. At that time, the Ötzi inquiry focused on:

1) Why was he at 10,530 feet (3210m) in the Alps alone?
2) What was the cause of his death?
3) Why was his death at this particular location?
4) Was he from a previously identified group of people?
5) Why was his equipment broken and scattered?
6) What was the cause of the odd wounds to his body?

Once the session work and drawings were completed, we compared McMoneagle's data with the lab reports and scientific abstracts released through the years. The Iceman is important because never before had a corpse this ancient been recovered that was not in burial clothing. Ötzi also provided scientists with the

Fotomasi

Italian Alps looking west through the Adige River Valley. In search of a new home, Ötzi's tribe probably migrated along the river (center left), up around the valley's bend to the north, where they passed by a Phase I Remedello community.

world's oldest DNA and Neolithic hunting equipment.

From Virginia, USA, Mr. McMoneagle acquired the target:

McMoneagle - First impressions are kind of weird. Get a very old person, who probably fell off the "'Ugly Wagon." ...appears to be a hunter/gatherer type of individual who seems to be exploring or something like that. What's interesting is the age; seems to be a lot older than I originally thought.

To guard against target revealing analytic overlay, from that point forward Ötzi's code name became "Mr. Ugly."

* * *

Alpine weather had been unusual during the Twentieth Century's eighth decade. Climate data confirms the Alps warmest ten-year interval was between 1982 and 1991. During the 1991 summer, the glaciers were in maximum retreat. As early as March the regions mean temperature averaged 3.5°C (38°F). Along with the melting temperatures, a heavy Saharan dust blew into the Southern Alps during March 5 - 8. The mountain snows turned yellowish and the sunlight burned deep into glacial ice.

This freakish Saharan dust re-appeared in July. The sun drove deeper into the ice causing the glaciers to recede further. At Ötzi's elevation, the average temperature rose to 5.6°C (40°F) and by mid-September an ancient body arose from the ice.

Alpine News Flash – Corpse discovered: "Alpine incident: body discovered at Hauslabjoch- preliminary report. On (Thursday) 19 September 1991 towards 12.00 (noon) mountaineers descending from Finalspitze (mountain), in the area of the Hauslabjoch, found a body half emerged from the glacier, almost upright in the ice. Only head and shoulders projecting from the ice. Markus Pirpamer, the keeper of the Similaunhutte, thereupon notified the (City of) Solden police. He was at the location himself in the afternoon. Judging by the equipment, this was an alpine accident going back many years. Recovery of the body is expected to take place on 20.09. 1991. A further report will be submitted."[xlv]

Ötzi's remains had been discovered at 3210 meters (3510 yards or 10,531 feet) by hikers in the Ötztal Alps. Once notified, the authorities approached the site as a crime scene.

Recovery operations started the next Monday. Due to the

corpse's condition, scientists concluded that at death the man must have been immediately covered with snow and held in the ice until his discovery for what turned out to be a rounded number of about 5,300 years or approximately 1,934,500 overnights. Solden's Dr. Edgar Wutscher was to issue the death certificate.

There have been varying estimates of Ötzi's physical size. When found, there was clear evidence of body mass atrophy making height and weight determinations controversial.

Ötzi had shrunk to 1.615 meters (5'3") weighting 14.97 kilos (33lbs). But his height is disputed by another scientific analysis incorrectly claiming Otzi was 1.58m (5'2").[xlvi] There have been three scientific age estimations of which McMoneagle acknowledges it is difficult to measure.

McMoneagle – Got a man who is approximately five feet, six in(ches) **tall** (1.70m)**. At time of death, he weighed in at about 160 pounds** (72.6 Kilos)**, give or take about ten. He was very strong and probably about 30 to 35 years of age. It's difficult to tell, as again, back when he was alive, I get a sense that no one lived to a ripe old age anyway.**[12]

Spindler: *"He had a strong physique, even though, as a result of his work in wind and weather, the first signs of wear and tear had begun to appear in his joints."*[xlvii] *"The degree of wear therefore provides a clue to the Iceman's age at death. The formula applied suggests, for the Iceman, a range from thirty-five to forty years."*[xlviii]

Scientists: "Determination of the iceman's age at death is difficult and inexact. Because all epiphyses (growth processes) were closed, the lowest estimate of age is young adulthood. Bone mineral content was excellent, and the lower-extremity (leg) long-bone cortices (structural outer layer) were particularly thick."[xlix] For some reason Ötzi's leg bones were thicker than normal Neoliths.

"While these features might favor a person in their 20s or 30s, it must be remembered that the iceman's life was probably spent in the Alps (non-agricultural), where exercise favored thick (leg) cortices as long as the person remained active.[13] Evidence of osteoarthritis and vascular calcification might favor an older age, perhaps 50s or 60s. However, a mountain lifestyle might acceler-

[12] A ten-pound variation puts the Iceman living weight as low as 150 lbs. or 68 kilos. Otzi's heavy muscularization accounts for the discrepancies in weight estimates.

[13] Author's underlining.

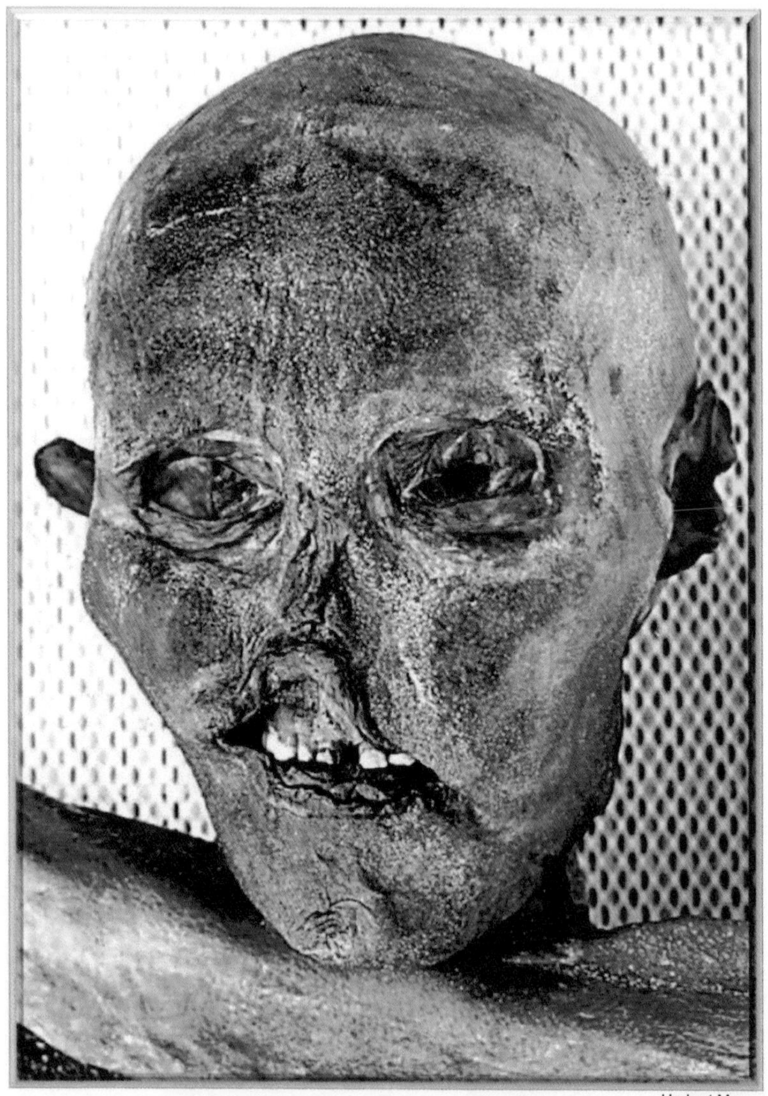

Herbert Maurer

Ötzi's Face Today

With his nose oddly smashed down, and after hitting the back of his skull on stone, Ötzi rolled onto his stomach, his arm up under his chin, went into a coma, and was quickly frozen. With his face down, pushing his lip up, his teeth can be seen. Was his left eye put out during the violent action that befell him?

McMoneagle RV Art – Evidential Details ©1998

Real Time Portrait

U.S. Military remote viewers were constantly tasked on drawing suspects faces. Colorized, his mouth, beard and hairline are shown beneath his bearskin hat.

ate wear and tear, and perhaps diet and/or genetic factors favored vascular calcification. Lacking better justification, 40–50 years of age seems a reasonable estimate for the iceman when he died."[I] Non pastoral thick leg bones imply climbing (Mesolithic) rather than agriculture (Neolithic). So what of Ötzi's appearance?

Spindler: *"Presently available methods do not make it possible to establish the Iceman's hairline and as this is a major factor in a person's appearance, we cannot make any detailed statements about the Iceman's face.*"[li]

Scientists: "Because of mummification and deformation due to environmental factors, the iceman's lips do not provide an accurate indication of his appearance during life."[lii]

McMoneagle - His skin is dark, but only from the sun. He has a very weathered sense about him. His eyes were very dark brown, hair was very dark brown as well, possibly black. Heavy features, but medium boned. He had a somewhat oval face with a larger than normal mouth and bad teeth. My sense is that he had a sort of scraggly beard. What I mean by that, is that he probably actually pulled facial hair from his face either by habit or in order to be more cleanly faced than not. There were some that he of course had to let grow in order to pull them out. It was probably a monthly occurrence. So there would have been fewer and fewer which would have grown out on a monthly basis - hence, scraggly beard (very little beard).

Scientists: "Of importance was the fact that nearly all occlusal (chewing) surfaces were worn smooth, and most teeth were shortened as a result. This feature was attributed to cultural factors, including diet and work habits believed to be operative in the period during which the iceman lived. Because of restricted jaw mobility due to dry and brittle tissue, it was not possible to obtain bitewing and periapical (root) dental images. Similarly, because of physical restrictions due to overall rigidity of the body, panoramic radiography was not practical. No tooth decay was evident at limited visual inspection or at imaging with non-dental methods."[liii]

Spindler: *"...great wear and tear is evident in the left frontal upper jaw. Such phenomena are known to dentists as functional wear and tear, unrelated to normal chewing action. The dental diagnosis of the Iceman suggests that his functional tooth wear is due to some habitual action which, unfortunately, we cannot ascertain.*"[liv]

McMoneagle - He was using his teeth to tear tendons from game to dry and use for string e.g., tying off the arrow points, tying bundles, or in the creation of snares for small animals. The only way to produce string from animal tendons is to chew (cut off a segment with your teeth), then grip that small segment and tear out the smaller string of tendon from

the larger. It takes a powerful jaw action to do that, which over time probably wears the teeth down on the side doing the gripping of the tendon material. Given that's his preferred side for tearing things, he probably formed a habit of chewing dried meat on that side as well, further complicating the wear action in that area of his teeth.

Scientists: "The worn incisors probably reflected use of the teeth as tools to work leather strips for clothing and other requirements. Saliva wets the leather, and the teeth act to soften and form the leather into the desired length and shape. Constant drawing of leather strips back and forth across the incisors would cause uniform wear."[lv]

As for determining Ötzi's epoch, American scientist Willard F. Libby, and his physicists, developed radio carbon dating during the years 1946-1947. Tests on Ötzi narrowed his life time to within a 325-year range. Further radiocarbon dating decreased the period to between 3,352 and 3,108 B.C., a 244 year spread. The Swedish laboratory analysis came in at 2800 B.C.

McMoneagle - I would say it was probably about 2500 years before Christ, give or take a couple of hundred; Probably somewhere between Stone Age and Iron Age - about half way perhaps. I think that there were probably some very rare, exceedingly rare people that lived at the time that might have discovered iron that could be hammered into something useful, but for the most part 99.9 percent were still relying on stone, flint, etc.

Alpine Incident Update - Austrian Police Station - Officer Schopf - "Body discovered at Hauslabjoch (Niederjochferner) - supplement. On 20.9.1991 District Inspector Koler of the Imst police was flown to the Hauslabjoch by the helicopter of the Federal Ministry of the Interior in order to effect the recovery of the body. Because of unfavorable weather conditions the recovery operation had to be cut short. It was only possible to free the corpse from the ice up to the region of its hips. The dead man's identity has not as yet been established. On the strength of the articles found near the body it may be assumed that the accident happened as long ago as the nineteenth century. Given appropriate weather conditions recovery will be continued and/or completed. When further details become known a report will again be submitted."[lvi]

Neolithic tribal roles generally involved age and health

status. What niche did the Iceman carve out as one of the older tribal members? Various anthropologists have speculated Ötzi was an outlaw, a shepherd, a shaman, a farmer or a prospector for metal ores. He may also have been traveling for trade or simply hunting. As Ötzi is one of the world's foremost archaeological discoveries. So we found archaeologists were prejudiced in favor of a positive notion of his circumstances. Previously, the oldest corpse discovered in the Alps had dated back to about 1595.

McMoneagle - What defines the past is not so much the bones, but our perception of them, the context in which we display them.[lvii]

He was single and a wanderer.[lviii] [14] **I get a sense that he was just simply unattached. Probably not young enough or strong enough to keep or possess a female by then. I have a sense that he was from a tribe of people who were wanderers. They spent most of their days wandering through forests of great trees. My sense is that he spent most of his days wandering, either in search of a new home, or because he had to for survival (hunter and gatherer). All nomadic. No agriculture, except for some very rare keeping of herbs. And the herbs kept were primarily medicinal.**

On Tuesday October 1, 1991, Ötzi achieved official status as a protected ancient monument and archeological questions went across the board. How and why were the strange wounds to his body inflicted? What were the events that led to his death? Why were his tools broken and scattered?

The same year as these sessions, the late Tom Loy of the Center for Molecular and Cellular Biology, University of Queensland in Brisbane, Australia, provided the most accurate portrayal long before it was acceptable. "The picture that emerges from my analysis of Ötzi's possessions is of a mature, highly skilled hunter – certainly not a shepherd." "This man was not just handy at repairs but was a craftsman who made the most of his mountain gear himself."[lix]

Scientists: "We can finally observe that although the com-

---

[14] In 1998, Mr. McMoneagle was the first to describe Ötzi as a "wanderer". This was then picked up by scientists for an abstract in the Journal of Human Evolution 51-1 (2006), entitled: *The Iceman's constitution was athletic, he was more a wanderer than a manual worker.* It was satisfying to see remote viewing language put into official usage dated eight years after our research.

position of his last meals offers no obvious contribution to the hypothesis on whether the Iceman was or was not the victim of a ritual sacrifice, the finding of ibex and deer meat certainly strengthens the one that, among other possible social roles, he covered that of hunter."[lx]

As determined by Mr. McMoneagle in 1998, by 2010 researchers had generally accepted that Ötzi had been a hunter. While his origin was still unknown, clues started to emerge as to how he died on the Italian - Austrian border.

Spindler: *"At some point about then a disaster must have occurred, whose nature, of course, as the Iceman is our only source of information, we cannot reconstruct. There was certainly a violent conflict..."*[lxi] *"The description of the Iceman's equipment ...provided very specific clues that, shortly before his death, the man must have suffered some disaster, an event associated with the action of considerable force."*[lxii] This would rule out a one inch arrowhead in the shoulder blade as the cause of death.

As it turned out, Ötzi's circumstances are actually at odds with what is generally thought about these early tribes. For example: "In these early societies...the elders enjoyed a special respect; it was generally conceded that an old age man was very clever, particularly favored by the gods, or just plain lucky. Whatever the reason for his longevity, his experience was useful to the tribe, for he often remembered what had been done in the past when the people had been confronted by unusual problems."[lxiii]

For reasons that will be detailed, we found that despite being nicely attired and having a copper axe, Ötzi was not wealthy and not a tribal leader. But, he did have a bachelor's accumulation of Neolithic assets. And he knew how to dress for acceptance in a Neolithic community.

Alpine Incident Update – On Saturday, September 21, 1991, the public prosecutor instructed the Solden police to deliver the body to the Institute of Forensic Medicine. No autopsy orders were issued. On Monday, September 23, 1991, the first helicopter rescue was attempted at 11:30 a.m. Just after 4:00 p.m. the body was delivered to Dr. Unterdorfer at the Forensic Medicinal Institute at Innsbruck. Taken to the dissection table, body (ref# 91/619) was attended by a Public Prosecutor, an Examining Magistrate and an Attorney. The doctor's statement said in part: "I have given instructions that the body should be handled with care and that there are no indications of third-party culpability or a culprit still pursuable. I have no objections to the corpse being photographed by the press, etc. Innsbruck, 23.9.1991."[lxiv]

Google Earth 3D (2015)

The Remedello Plain from the raised Langtaufers Valley entrance. One can imagine Otzi's panorama looking out at wooden Neolithic long huts, people and livestock in motion, planted fields and furnace smoke where the lake is now.

Origin

Herkunft

Origine

As of this printing, Ötzi's birth site remained unknown. But, scientists wanted evidence connecting the mummy to an identified Neolithic group like the Tamis-Carasso-Isera. But Ötzi is actually more historically significant as being from an unidentified tribe.

Most scholars believed Ötzi's journey started into the Alps from the south. But using McMoneagle's maps, we drew different conclusions. Since 1998, ours has been single premise indicating Ötzi entered the Hochjoch pass from the north. Excerpting McMoneagle's map and clues (bold text), we were able to determine Ötzi's adult home base. The clues were:

1) That Ötzi died a "**distance from** (his) **village about 25 miles**" travelling **"from West to East generally speaking;"**
2) That his home camp is in a, **"high mountain valley"**, **"to one side of the mountain range"**, **"just off"** a main trail and that it must be at some elevation, "**because it is mostly a cooler or cold climate;"**
3) That, **"The entire population of this tribe is probably about sixty people total;"**
4) That this mountain valley offers a finite food resource as, **"It is getting harder and harder to find game where they currently reside;"**
5) That this valley must include, **"mountain springs and a small waterfall;"**
6) That it must be within another tribe's range that confronts Ötzi's tribe as he was seeking a place, **"where the game was good, and there were no other tribes to contend with or compete with for the food source."**

McMoneagle – He is most definitely a hunter and gatherer. His camp was in a valley to one side of the mountain range. I suspect like a high alpine valley.

The Alp's highest valley is the Langtaufers Valley. But who was the Neolithic group living in the adjacent Val Venosta Valley? The Archeology Department Chairman at the University of Austria, Innsbruck, then Dr. Walter Leitner, responded:

Generally, it is to be assumed that the earliest phase of the remedello-culture was prevalent.[lxv]

This would be Phase I Remedello, a two-staged Copper and Bronze Age people living in northern Italy and Switzerland. This cultivational society existed from 3200 to about 2800 B.C. Ötzi's axe was flanged similarly to Remedello artifacts, so we acknowledged that group. That society's name does not impact Ötzi's story. But it is most likely the origin of his copper head axe.

The Langtaufers Valley is on the Val Venosta Valley's northeast side. In the 2001 census, the Valley population was 446. The total area is 107.5 square kilometers, or 41.5 square miles of what was dense forest. Today it is bi-lingual German and Italian.

"The Langtaufers Valley is one of the most primitive valleys of the Alps and shows still a largely unspoiled mountain farming landscape. From the Langtauferstal (Langtaufer Valley) in from

Image by Get Magic

The Remedello's Valley looking west. Coming from the south (left) Ötzi's tribal scouts found the Alp's highest, coldest and driest valley unoccupied. The tribe travelled past a Neolithic fishing village at the smaller lake, and settled in the curved back half of the Langtaufers Valley (lower right corner). This new settlement's location would only last about as long as the rest of Otzi's life.

Courtesy Sandro Brasso

Looking east at Curon Venosta in the Langtaufers Valley entrance. They arrived from the right (south) during Ötzi's adolescence. His final journey began at the valley's far end. Lake Resia now covers a large Neolithic village in what is known today as the Val Venosta Valley. This is where Ötzi got his equipment and clothing.

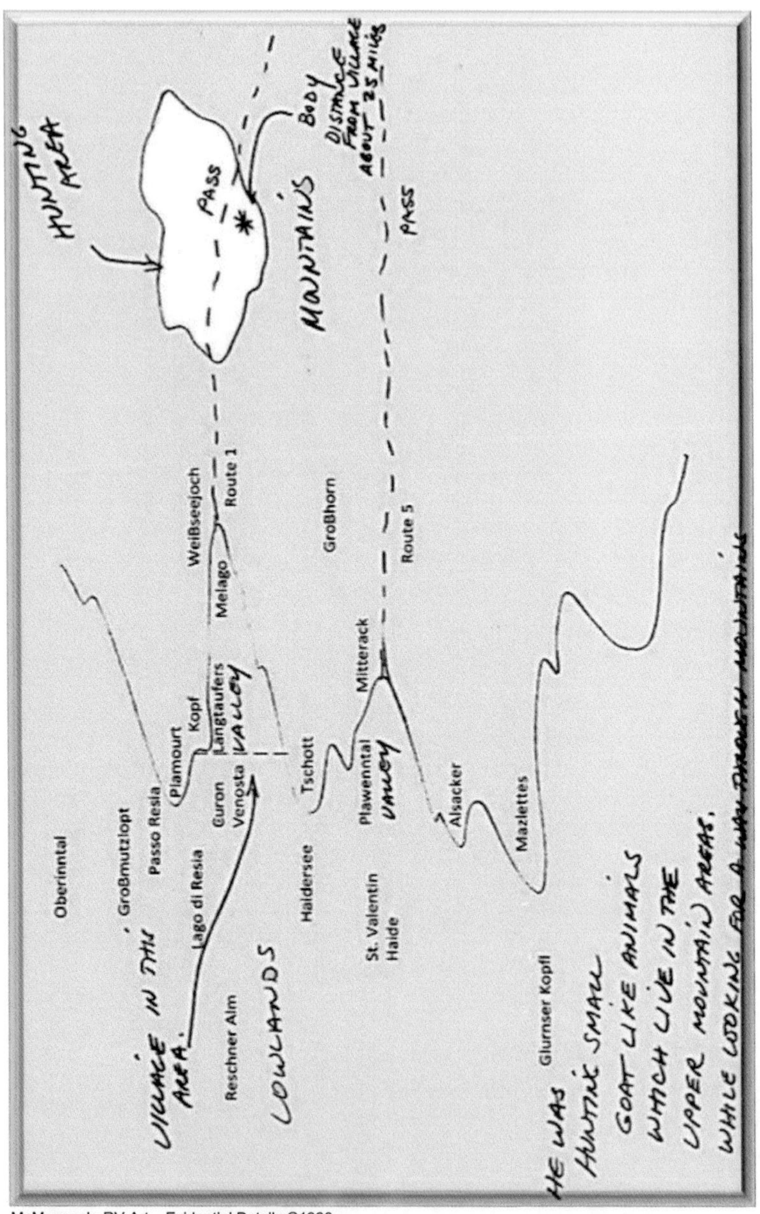

McMoneagle RV Art – Evidential Details ©1998

This map shows Ötzi's previously unknown origin. The geographical contours established the Langtaufers Valley as his origin point. **Lowlands** (left center) refers to the real time valley subsequently covered by Lake Resia. Of interest is the width of McMoneagle's **Hunting Area** (white area top right) which turned out to be on both sides of the town of Vent, Austria (typed labels and colorization by author), the Graun (Curon Venosta) a very good road leads to Melag(o). Karli creek flows directly into the Reschensee." (Lake Resia)[lxvi]

Feedback Question: "Do you recall if there was any source of water for Mr. Ugly's village?"

McMoneagle – Yes, mountain springs and a small waterfall. My sense is that the waterfall is not very large at all in terms of how far the water falls. However, it is a series actually of more than one, none greater than probably the height of a man, or perhaps ten feet. The overall size is probably something on the range (length) **of 300 to 350 feet overall -- top to bottom.**

Alpenwelt-travel.com

The Langtaufers Valley's Karli Brook looking east. A cascading waterfall emerges (**blue arrow**). Notice the ground's slant toward the creek.

We had concerns about a 5,300 year old waterfall still existing. But in an amazing development, once we lighten the Karli Brook tree shadows, a cascade, about as tall as a man each, appeared south of Kappl, Italy at 1860m/6102ft.

This evidential detail validated McMoneagle's data and identified Ötzi's base camp location. "The Karli creek is a 19. 6 km (12.2 mile) long tributary of Lake Resia in South Tyrol."[lxvii] Listening to these falls is to share the ambience Ötzi's tribe enjoyed, and will one day be a stop on any historian's tour. Our research model assumed that Ötzi's hunter-gatherer tribe needed the entire Langtaufers Valley's for forage.

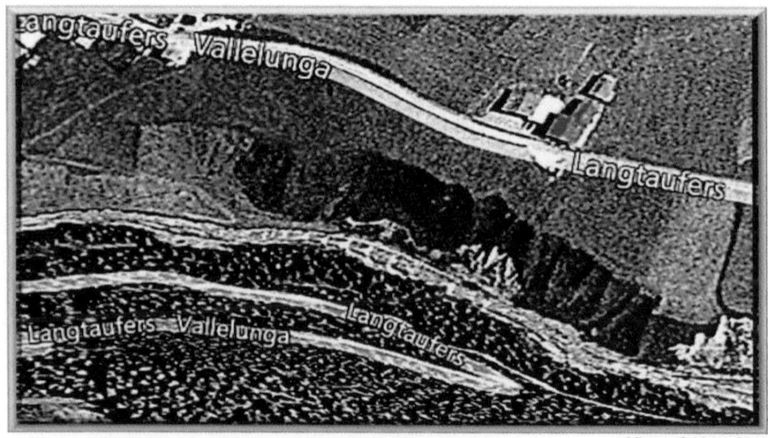

Microsoft Maps 2013

With the trees along the south side of the brook, a soothing cascading falls (center) is likely the area Ötzi's tribe came to the river.

Feedback Question: *In your opinion, would it be possible for anthropologists to reconstruct backward motion out of the Alps along known paths that would narrow the research required to establish his home territory?*

McMoneagle – My opinion is yes. They should be able to back track him on known paths to his place of origin. I believe his place of origin was a valley, which was very close to the primary mountain path he took to (ultimately) **cross to the south. All brand new. He was essentially exploring. I think to search out new fields of game.**

It is known the Val Venosta Valley was favorable to settlement and that it had first become populated about in the Fifth Millennium B.C. The first forest clearances started around 4,000 B.C. In 1950, the Italian Government demolished the town of Curon Venosta and had it rebuilt in the Langtaufers Valley entrance. As the waters rose to create a military obstacle power reservoir. The partially submerged bell-tower became a landmark and emblem.

The Langtaufers Valley is the coldest valley in the Alps - too cold for most people to want to stay. Here the forest was dense, and the hunting good enough to provide for a 60 person clan. But it was not farmable, so there could be no ongoing hunting adversarialism without risking a flat lined tribe under constant risk of intermittent starvation. A territorial defense would be needed. And these fleeting Mesoliths would need every warrior.

Wikipedia Commons

The landmark sunken church steeple, in Lake Resia, is where the previous town stood. The entrance to the Langtaufers Valley (center) gives historians a sense of what it would be like to see Ötzi walk down the hill into the valley to trade. His view can be seen on page 54.

As Ötzi headed into adulthood, he found himself in a cold secluded valley where his people enjoyed relative autonomy for a couple of decades. But the Remedello may have been hunting in the Langtaufers Valley when Ötzi's tribe arrived. Ötzi realized time was not on the side of his pre-Neolithic tribe, so he became interested in the people that had forced his tribe to move with great suffering and loss.

As the Remedello numbers increased, their hunters had to climb into the mountains and at great labor carry out game. Or, they could hunt for multiple species in what was essentially the Langtaufers Valley game preserve. The stage was set for events archaeologists admittedly know little about. As fields were plowed and harvested, furnaces fueled, and livestock milked, Ötzi compared cultures and understood what had happened when he was a young man. He wanted what the Neoliths had. But could he gain acceptance?

McMoneagle - However, alone, one could get away with just sort of showing up and trading with the tribe who controlled the area. In other words, they were threatened by large groups but not by individuals.

Ötzi probably approached the Remedello Community with pelts for barter. With these clothes he imaged as a Neolith. Did Ötzi work in the valley? It accounts for his axe, his accouterments, apparel and, as we will see, why his people were cool toward him.

Behind the bell tower lays the entrance to the Lantaufers Valley. Here Remedello hunters started up into the Langtaufers Valley. It was inevitable Ötzi's tribe would encounter them while hunting. It is likely an intermittent type of "no man's land" struggle ensued when the two groups came upon each other at different points in the primeval forest. Ötzi was likelly apprehensive to shoot arrows in either direction. He may have recognized some of the Remedello fighters. Should he shoot at the future or the past?

Ötzi must have come to the conclusion that the Mesolithic way of life was behind, and the tribe saw this in him as well. Ötzi would eventually be torn between more than just two villages. He was torn between two epochs. But he still needed to prove himself to his boyhood tribe. It may have been a "*don't forget where you came from*" attitude that characterized his last journey. So, just as his tribal elders had done two decades earlier, in Neolithic clothing, Ötzi was sent out to look for another place for his tribe to settle.

Village Life & Times

Dorfleben & Zeit

La Vita & Tempo di Villaggio

The timberline in the Italian Alps is close to the 2200 meter (7,218ft) contour on its Southern slope, which is just 340m (1,115ft) above Kappl, Italy. Once inhabited by Ötzi's tribe, it has been deforested. We refer to them as the Langtaufer people.

Scientists: "After the end of the last Glacial period, the altitudinal zonation of the forests became progressively established: (**i**) mixed deciduous forest (oak, elm, lime, ash, maple, and hornbeam) in the valleys; (**ii**) mixed deciduous and coniferous forest (spruce, fir, beech, hazel, birch, and other deciduous species) at intermediate altitudes; and (**iii**) subalpine coniferous forest (Arolla pine, dwarf mountain pine, Scots pine, larch, and spruce) up to the tree line. With regard to the ferns, these plants grow in moist habitats of the Alps in a wide range of low and intermediate altitudes."

"If we now consider the...DNA spectrum of the (his) colon and the pollen spectrum...we can observe that both fit with the distribution of the above-described vegetation... (and) they apparently correspond to different altitudinal zones of vegetation."[lxviii] As McMoneagle pointed out four years earlier, this confirmed Ötzi had not remained in one vegetation zone prior to his death.

Scientists: "A reasonable hypothesis is that the iceman was part of a population that was well aware of injuries caused by the cold."[lxix]

McMoneagle – The entire population of this tribe is

probably about sixty people total. I think that heavy log and skin huts are the primary way they live in his village. ...skin covered hovels, which are somewhat circular, are what he uses and others like him when they are away from the village and need to set up a mid-range base camp; like on long hunting trips, that sort of thing; ...primarily skin covered hovels, which are...made with green saplings stuck in the ground, are bowed over one over-lapping the next. Skins are not well processed, but the fur is left on them and they are worn inside out in winter, fur side out in summer or spring. They have fire inside, because it is mostly a cooler or cold climate.

"Hovels." Mesolithic communities are generally depicted with round top housing of the kind McMoneagle described. The people above are also depicted without pottery.

As the Neolithic population grew, and the 220 acre (89 hector) Lake Haidersee fishing stocks dwindled, the Remedello needed to find supplemental food sources. Besides birds, Ibex and rodents, the tribesmen would have encountered marmot, deer, bear, fox, wild boar and wolves. Over time, the Remedello and Ötzi's tribe certainly viewed each other as food competitors.

As the Remedello drove deeper into the Langtaufers Valley, Ötzi's tribe needed to keep them out to maintain their quality of life. So confrontations, likely along the Karli Brook path, brought the tribe's numerically superior adversaries closer. As in modern times, the Remedello probably viewed Ötzi's people as resource depleting immigrants of twenty years ago who never belonged there. If so, in time the competition for game may have taken on a contemptuous aspect, perhaps with malice.

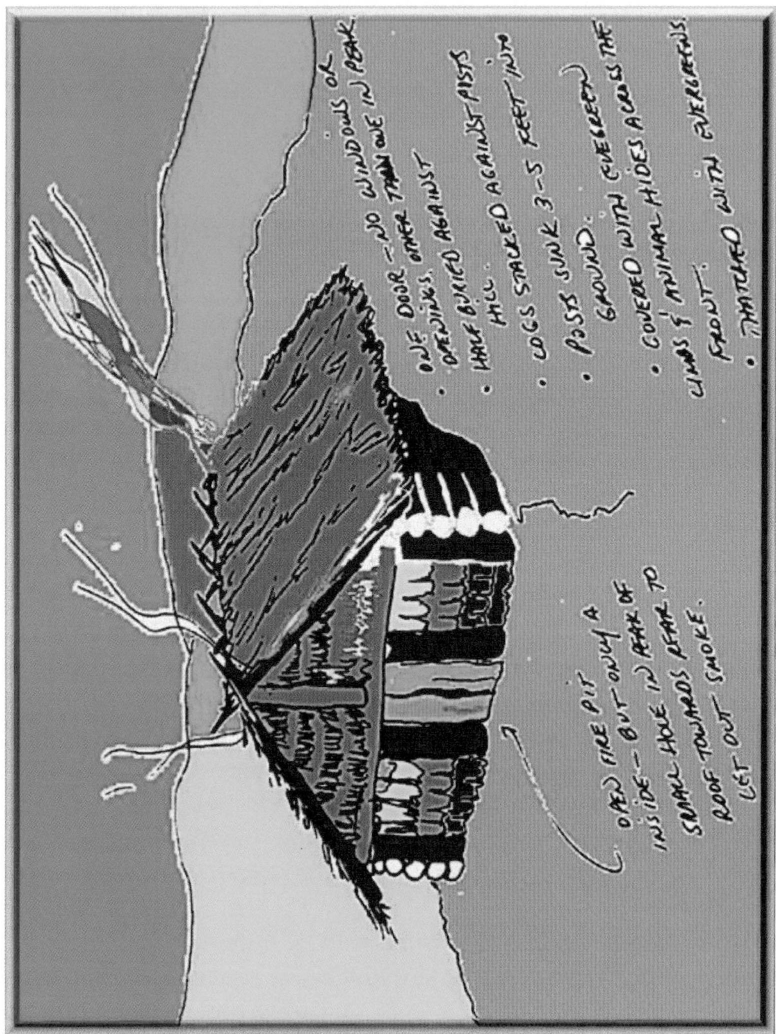

McMoneagle RV Art – Evidential Details ©1998

Ötzi's Hut

Military Remote Viewers were frequently tasked with drawing a suspect's hideout. This is where Ötzi lived. The notes read: ***Open Fire Pit Inside – But Only a Small Hole in Peak of Roof Towards Rear to let Out Smoke. One Door – No Windows, Half Buried Against Hill, Logs Stacked Against Posts, Post Sunk 3-5 Feet into Ground, Covered with Evergreen Limbs & Animal Hides Across the Front, Thatched with Evergreens.*** Fashioned on the front end of a Neolithic long house, notice the sharpened cross bars along the roof and the vertical king post truss above the door. We found it interesting that, once determined years later, this image showed the Langtaufers valley floor on the same slant toward the Karli Brook (Colorized by author).

As their westbound hunting range became dangerous, the tribe looked east for mountain goats and finally a new place to live. In the end, they may have been bottled up with no Western escape without facing the larger, heavier, copper armed Remedello and their extended range long bows.

McMoneagle - I think it was very primitive. They would steal from one another if they had superior numbers. Probably had something to do with food sources and good territory for scrounging nuts, berries, roots, etc.

They don't have any code external to the tribe. They have a good deal of respect for one another, but no respect for anything outside of their tribal unit. I think these people are tolerant and kind to one another, but not to outsiders; they probably only see outsiders on a rare occasion.

Militarily, it's a crap shoot. They would probably attack any other tribe they ran into, simply because they have to compete for food sources. I think he probably had killed others before. Perhaps a fight between tribes, where he thought he was defending his own. I don't think he was a soldier. But, he may have actually been acting in that capacity, at least as a watcher (scout) **of one of the out areas away from his tribal area. I do get more of a sense that he was searching for or looking for a new area that his tribe could move to.**

"Unpublished and thus unconfirmed DNA analyses claim they revealed traces of blood from four other people on his (Ötzi's) gear: one from his knife, two from the same arrowhead, and a fourth from his coat."[lxx]

McMoneagle - Their form of communication seems to be very primitive, mostly single words, lots of hand motions, and grunts. I also get a sense that they had a very sophisticated whistling system for hunting, so they could coordinate the encirclement of game by large groups of hunters.

Scientists: "There is no direct evidence of the languages spoken in the Neolithic. Some proponents of paleolinguistics attempt to extend the methods of historical linguistics to the Stone Age, but this has little academic support."[lxxi]

McMoneagle - Tribal life was somewhat sophisticated. There are elders who make decisions that the rest of the tribe have to live with.

In archaeology, pottery is a primary research tool. It helps determine to which tribe a particular group of people or individual belonged. We wondered if the Iceman's tribe could be identified through any pottery currently in world collections.

Feedback Question: "Any pottery for cooking?"

McMoneagle - Negative. They cook with rocks, on rocks, and inside shells.

Feedback Question: "Do you think there was a shaman in the tribe?"

McMoneagle - Yes. Probably female.

Feedback Question: "Because of his age, was 'Ugly' considered an elder within the village?"

McMoneagle - No. I don't think so. I do believe he was viewed as a great hunter and explorer though.

Ötzi's copper axe is not a clue to his tribal status. To the tribe it was possibly a negative Neolithic metallurgical symbol.

"An elementary division of labor based on sex was common to many primitive societies. While men hunted and fished, made weapons, and fought the battles of the tribe, the women bore children, gathered roots and berries, and made clothes and baskets. ...we do know that the women began to make small garden plots, though their activity was necessarily sporadic at first because of the migratory habits of the primitive tribes."[lxxii]

McMoneagle - The women are hardy, and their jobs seem to center around gathering. They spend most of their time gathering herbs and roots or tubers. They also spend a lot of time taking care of the young, sort of a group care effort actually, and making and tending to a fire.

I think some of the women probably felt they should pay particular attention to individual males, only because those males were strong enough and tough enough to provide for them. In other words, they all probably showed some preference one for the other, male and female alike. The women are traded or voluntarily move from tribe to tribe.

I don't think there was marriage because the concept just wasn't fully understood. I do not get a sense of marriage, but more of communal sharing. The women and men do not understand the connection between sex and child production, but they do have a very protective caring for the children.

"...the quite primitive mother seldom bothered to inquire into the paternity of her child; it belonged to her, and she belonged not to a husband but to her father—or her Brother - and the clan;"[lxxiii] "Women, apart from her biological disabilities, was almost the equal of man in stature, endurance, resourcefulness and courage; she was not yet an ornament, (or) a thing of beauty ...she was...able to perform arduous work for long hours, and if necessary, to fight to the death for her children of her clan."[lxxiv]

McMoneagle - Infant survival is only about twenty-five percent unfortunately. The women breast feed, and there is always more than one wet nurse among the tribe. They don't much care which child they are feeding. Young children have their food chewed by the older women. The older women also pre-chew the food for the older men as well. Problems with teeth actually are a very serious thing in this tribe. It is probably the single greatest killer (starvation) of these people aside from accidental death; which is what I sense this guy probably died from.

"It was she who developed the home, slowly adding man to the list of her domesticated animals, and training him in those social dispositions and amenities which are the psychological basis and cement of civilization."[lxxv]

McMoneagle - They are spiritual in a sense that they have animistic beliefs. They are pretty sure that good and bad spirits inhabit their world. Everything has a spirit in it, and the spirit can be good or bad. They are afraid of the dark and spirits reside in everything: rocks, trees, earth, caves, people, animals, etc. They don't pray to any of them, but they do keep records on skins.

I can see them sitting around the fire and making dyed impressions on smooth skins which have had the hair removed. It is a very specific record of their history, important hunts, or special occasions they mark time with; like excessive snowfalls, periods of hunger or great loss, successful hunts, etc. The women are tasked with helping in the treatment of skins, but this is a task equally shared around the fire by the men as well.

This record keeping system came down through the millennia and was still in use as late as the 19th century. But Ötzi's Tribe does not fit the nomadic stereotype. These people seem to be at a permanent location and were simply being squeezed out.

"In the first centuries of the third millennium B.C., a surprising change occurred in Europe. Most people appear to have begun to follow a single religion and a new social system seems to have evolved, giving greater freedom and rights of personal ownership to the individual."[lxxvi] The Langtaufer people had not entered into this transition – but Ötzi may have attempted to.

Spindler: "*...the find in itself offers no basis for deciding whether the Iceman had anything to do with the keeping of domestic animals.*"[lxxvii]

McMoneagle - Do not get a sense of any domesticated animals. The only pets they kept were whatever they found in a very young state. Puppies mostly which they use as sort of an early warning device, and I get a sense they might have had a small black bear at one time or another, mostly for amusement. At least until it was eating size. The idea of keeping and caring for or feeding animals for any reason I think was pretty much beyond them. Although there may have been a couple of sister tribes which kept goats for milk. I think this guy (Ötzi among the Remedello) **would have had knowledge of that sort of thing. But, no his tribe didn't keep them.**

The bear cub was likely with a mother bear they killed. Bear fur was the warmest animal skin available.

Feedback Question: "Did you sense evidence of the wheel or of horses?"

McMoneagle - I do not believe they had either. The only animal sense I get is "mountain goats".

Feedback Question: "Any sense of these people's burial rites. If 'Ugly' had been found, would he have gotten a ceremonial burial?"

McMoneagle - I think so. I think they understand that man probably lives beyond death and they spend a bit of time planning out their funerals. Basically, buried in a shallow grave covered with stones, head pointing to the north, maybe some flower petals spread over his body. He most definitely would have been buried with some of his stuff like flints and things like that. But, a really good knife, no. Someone would have taken that. He most likely would have been buried at or near the entrance to a cave or holy spot. His (Neolithic) **clothing would also have been taken as it was considered to be of very good value.**

Due to these circumstances, Ötzi, cloaked in his best Neo-garb, went over the Langtaufers Valley's eastern mountain ridge.

Virtual Neolithic Valley

Family hoe plots. Ötzi looked out onto the Remedello lands, realized what agriculture meant, and that his tribe could not compete. It was time for these Mesoliths to move again, but where could they go to get away from the larger, more numerous, higher technology, better nourished Neoliths wielding higher-tech weapons?

He was to find a new place for the clan to settle from which he may have been a near exile. He was suspect because of his time away; Neolithic interests; dress; his singular log cabin; a foundry based copper head axe; and his extended range Remedello longbow project nearing completion. He had become a Neolith in all but ancestry. His Langlaufers Tribe was "out gunned", in hovels, chipping stone. They needed every productive hunter they could muster, but increasingly Ötzi was with the Remedello.

When it was men against the mountain wilds, scouts went out in twosomes. This was to ensure that if someone got in trouble, a tribesman would be there to help. But when Otzi went out to explore into the unknown wilderness - he went alone.

The Journey

Die Reise

Il Viaggio

In 1273 the first Holy Roman King came to power in what is known to history as the Austro-Hungarian Empire. Rudolf I (1218 - 1291) was the Hapsburg Dynasty's first ruler over a kingdom that lasted 645 years. But Austrian control of the Ötztal Alps ended after the World War I Armistice took effect on November 11, 1918. In the 1922 Treaty of St. Germain-en-Laye, Austria was forced to cede this Alps range to Italy. The new Austria-Italy border was defined as the Rivers Inn and Etsch watershed.

When Ötzi was on today's Italian-Austrian border he died. Five millennia later these World War I treaty terms became the legal jurisdictional component in his guardianship. Ötzi was found in 1991, but for the first time since 1918, Austrians returned to their

McMoneagle - I believe his place of origin was a valley, which was very close to the primary mountain path he took... Here the historian can see Lake Resia (**left**) and the length of Italy's Langtaufers valley. This is the path (**right center**) that Ötzi's journey began. Kappl has a stream (moat) for protection on its west side. The purple line shows the modern Austrian/Italian border (**top left and right corners**).

historic land and stood guard over him inside modern Italy. It was these redrawn borders, 5,300 years after Ötzi's death that determined his final resting place. Though he was an Austrian recovery, the Ice-man would ultimately find his home in Bolzano, Italy. With a population of ~100,000, the city is the Trentino-Alto Adige provincial capital, north-northwest of Venice.

Based on the artifacts, on Wednesday, September 25, 1991, the Austrian Provincial Public Health Director impounded Ötzi's body while still on the mountain. Then Italian authorities appeared claiming the body had been discovered on Italian soil. Ultimately, military surveyors determined the Iceman was 92.56 meters (304ft) into Italy. The mountain ridge is 3,283m (10,771ft) above sea level. Ötzi was found at 3,209.8m (10,531ft).

McMoneagle – He was sent out as one of a number of scouts. His and the other scout's jobs were to find new areas in which the tribe could settle for long periods, where the game was good, and there were no other tribes to contend with or compete with for the food source.

Scientists confirmed Ötzi was not in good physical condition for his trip. He was found with Whipworm eggs (*Trichuris trichiura*) in his colon which causes stomachache and diarrhea. He also had some arthritis, lime disease, and was lactose intolerant.

Scientists: "Similarly, there is evidence of mild osteoarthritis in the right sacroiliac joint and right hip joint. Even though we do not know the cause of the arthritis, we can speculate that the degenerative changes of the spine and hip were probably painful."[lxxviii] "However, the C 6–7 (Cervical - the top seven neck bones)) disk space was slightly narrower than the others, and this finding was associated with mild endplate sclerosis (hardening) with dorsal and ventral spurs. These features satisfied diagnostic criteria for degenerative disk disease."[lxxix] "These features were attributed to osteoarthritis. They appeared consistent with the degenerative alterations found in the spine, which served as confirmation that the iceman had acquired degenerative arthritis during his life."[lxxx]

Feedback Question: Do you have any sense or remembrance about the ease of the Iceman's movement into the mountains? Was this guy using ancient trials and paths to move from his home village, or was he hacking his way through the forest?

McMoneagle – He was on a common trail. It was a ma-

jor trek though, especially in his condition. I believe he was either off on a hunt for a better place for his tribe, or he was driven out of the tribe because he was no longer welcome (banishment?)**. So, in either case, he was traveling alone and not under the best of conditions.**

Though humanity's migrated was westward, Ötzi's east-bound trek allowed for few path variations. Specifically, he departed the Langtaufers Valley east passing by today's Weisskugel Hutte grounds up to the Langtaufer Ferner. Continuing east, he passed through the Langtauferjoch between the Langtauferser Spitz (3229m/10,594ft) and the Hock Vernagl Wand (3435m/ 11,270), crossing into modern Austria which took him onto the Hintereist Ferner. Here he encountered a glacial water runoff and turned north on to modern trail 902.02. He continued north northeast into the river valley just south of the 919 trail junction.

Next, he crossed trail junction 902 leading north toward the town of Vent. This is a "medium challenge" trail. Hiking time from Kappl, Italy to Vent, Austria is about ten hours. But how fast Ötzi was progressing as a cautious explorer is unknown.

Likely staying on the Ventertal stream's west side, he moved north downhill on trail 902 into the Rofen forest perhaps going as far as the trail 920 junction (2014m/6,607ft). That would put him someplace southwest of Rofen probably near the end of the modern ski lift called DSB Wildspitze. At 460m/1,509ft above Vent, he probably saw camp fire smoke rising from the tree line.

"Archaeological discoveries near Vent prove that this region was the hunting ground for foragers in the Mesolithic period as early as 8,000 BC. During the summer months, they would camp at the entrance of the Rofantal and below the "Hohle Stein" rock fall just above Vent. Several fireplaces and numerous tools made of finely worked flintstone blades point to an active camp life."[lxxxi] This means the area where the two streams meet, may have been settled for 4,700 years before Ötzi arrived.

McMoneagle - I get a sense that while he was on his trek, he would probably avoid other tribes like the plague.

Stymied, Otzi headed back up south in the direction of the Schnalstal. Passing the 902,02 trail junction again, but wanting to get east, he came upon an east bound path. This was the trail over the dangerous Kreuzspitze peak (3459m/11,348ft), the highest in the Schnalskam group of the Ötztal Alps.

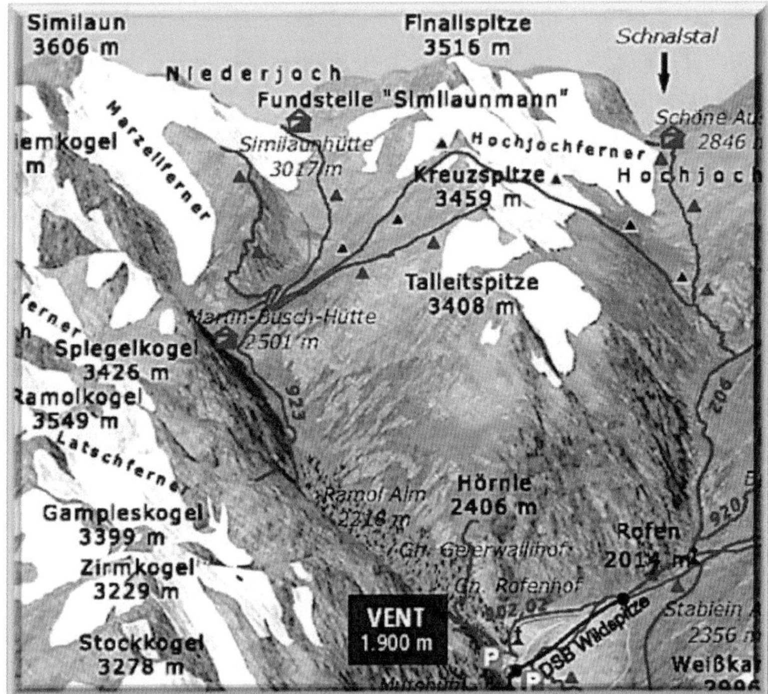

www.Soelden.com

Looking up South. Left is east. Ötzi travelled the rough path down toward **Rofen** on **trail 902** (right side). Encountering inhabitants, he went back up the trail and then over the red Kreuzspitze Mountain trail **(center)** which shows black & yellow triangular warning signs. The "**significant ridgelines**" McMoneagle reported were found to be the five named "Kogels" along the lower left side.

McMoneagle - I think he was headed from West to East generally speaking; moving through a system of mountains that essentially run in sort of an inverted 'V' lower left leg running southwest to northeast and right leg running from southeast to northwest. His direction of travel would be like a cross bar on the letter "A" going from West to East. (He) **Was moderately into them** (mountains), **but probably had not yet passed the key or significant ridgelines** (Kogels).

At 1896m/6,220ft, Vent, Austria turned out to be at the point of McMoneagle's "**V**". The eastbound Kreuzspitze trail turned out to be the crossbar on the "**A**" to which McMoneagle referred.

Once over the mountain, Ötzi came to the 923 trail junction and explored north again. Now on a medium challenge trail he headed into the Ramol Alm (2,218m/7,277ft) but encountered the same inhabitants in and around Vent from the other side.

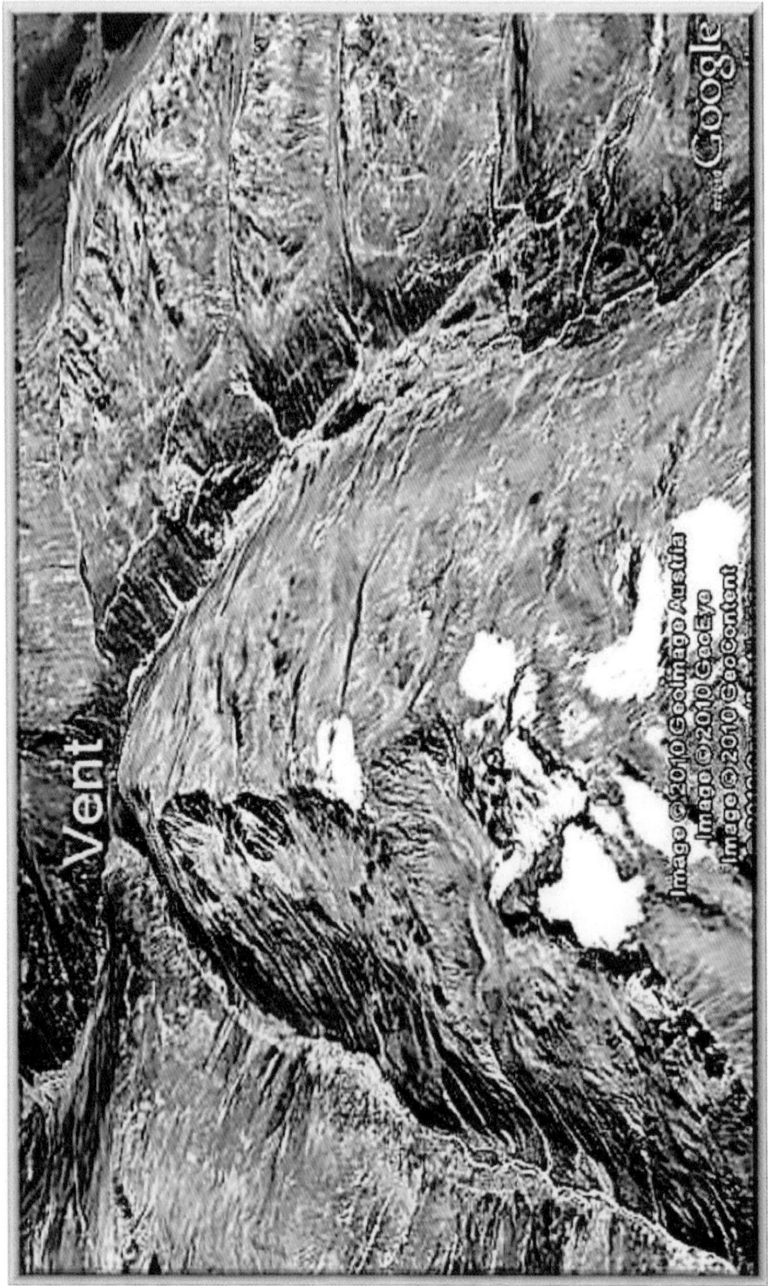

©2010Google Earth 3D

Looking north. We were stunned when the sides of the capital letter A appeared in the mountains. The Kreuzspitze Peak (center) is the closest snowcap to Vent. Ötzi crossed left to right (West to East) which is McMoneagle's capital letter A crossbar.

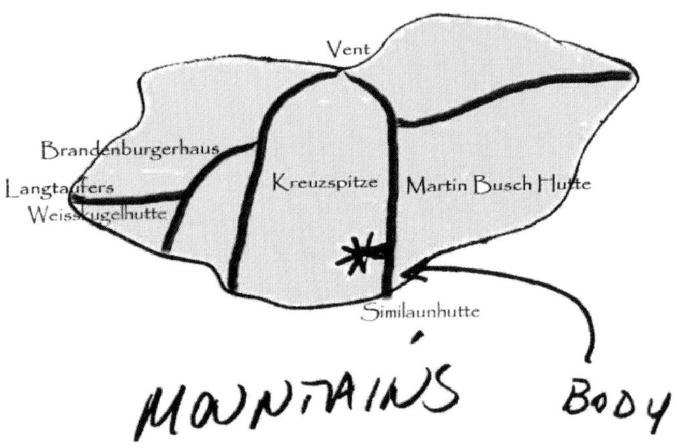

McMoneagle RV Art – Evidential Details ©1998
From the map on page 58. After inserting the names, the trails and the projected hiking routes, we saw a large explored area to the right (east) of Vent (top) in an area with no trails. But Ötzi's searching the eastern ridges made sense.

Once on Vent's east side, Ötzi looked for a way around the inhabitants. From Vent to the Ramol Alm is about a kilometer and can be hiked in about 45 minutes. But did the terrain allow for an exploration that wide? We went back to the maps.

When we searched, it was clear Ötzi could have gone east to get a look over the mountains ridges (Kogels). He needed to determine if there was any way a whole tribe could migrate over the eastern mountain ridges. From the top, he could look over to see if anything looked promising.

According to McMoneagle's map, and given his task, Ötzi went across the trail 923 stream and into the mountain to see if any possibilities existed. But there was no way for a his tribe to pass through these ridges. He must have been disappointed to realize he had to go back up south toward the Kreuzspitze trail intersection. From McMoneagle's map it appears he probably explored up the various eastern watershed streams along the way. But is there any verification of this type of movement?

Scientists: "Oddly enough, we believe he came back down (the mountain) again because there is another layer of hornbeam pollen on top of the conifer pollen, which means that he went up, for some reason came back down, and then back up again to his death."[lxxxii]

Google Earth 3D

These are the ridgelines (Kogels) McMoneagle referred to (top). Ötzi skirted the village at Vent (bottom center) by climbing the eastern mountains to see if there was passage. There were none that the women and children could be expected to negotiate along with all their processions.

McMoneagle - My sense is that he wasn't starving, but he was hunting... He was evidently hunting some kind of a deer or mountain goat, which has small pointed horns. A smaller rather than larger animal and one that spends a great deal of time in or on the rocks.

Ötzi explored the area southbound for a few days and made provisions. He may have made bread from the einkorn flour he brought. He did not know how long the hike would last or where it would lead. Because Norway maple leaves were found inside the Birch bark container, we know he had fresh leaves with chlorophyll. The stems were missing, so he may have taken the fresh, soft stems and made a "forest salad" or boiled them in water with meat to make porridge. "The first show that the plant 18S rDNA spectrum of the colon is dominated (73%) by the DNA of conifers, followed (22%) by that of cereals (Triticeae) and (5%) of ferns (Filicales)."

Scientists: "By using CT images as a map, a small stool sample was obtained. Evaluation showed that the iceman's recent diet consisted of unleavened bread made from finely ground einkorn wheat. The tiny particles of charcoal associated with the bran suggested a baking process. Fragments of muscle fiber and burned bone indicated that meat was part of a recent meal

He used his only workable 1.04 meter (41in) bow to kill a mountain goat he came upon while heading south toward the Niederjoch. Along the way he also killed, butchered, and roasted a deer while preserving some venison for the journey.

Scientists: "According to the DNA reconstruction, the man's last meal was composed of red deer (*Cervus elaphus*) meat, and, possibly, cereals; this meal had been preceded by another one based on ibex (*Capra ibex*), different species of dicots, and cereals. The DNA spectrum corresponding to pollen residues in the colon, on the other hand, fits with the hypothesis that the last journey of the Neolithic hunter/warrior was made through a subalpine coniferous forest to the site at over 3,200m above sea level, where his mummified body was to be discovered 5,000 years later."[lxxxiii] He went back down to the sub-alpine trail 923.

McMoneagle - I believe he was actually traveling from the Northwest to the Southeast. He was on a well-known path (923) **to the south through the mountains though.**

Scientists: "We are now able to demonstrate that although the use of ibex meat is confirmed by the result of the analyses of the colon content, the last meal of the Tyrolean Iceman was actually composed of red deer meat."[lxxxiv] "The use of red deer meat as a food supply is perfectly consistent with the paleozoological identification of the materials used by the iceman to manufacture his equipment:"[lxxxv]

Approaching the modern Martin-Busch Hütte grounds, (2,501m/8,205ft) about a 2.5 hour hike from Vent, Otzi cannot go east or north, or west toward where he started. And because of his tough experience going over the Kreuzspitze, he opted not to take on the difficult looking Marzellferner trail to the southeast. His only choice was to continue south to see what was over the Niederjoch ridge. This is the path to the Schnalstal mountain pass. "The Hochjoch is a transition in the Ötztal Alps, with a height of 2770m (9,088ft) above sea level. It connects the Senales with the Ötztal and Vent."[lxxxvi]

"The tour from Martin-Busch-Hütte to Similaunhütte leads along Niederjoch brook into the Niedertal. The trail then climbs gently through moraines. From (the) Seibach River you stay on the moraine ridge all the way to "Bild". After (the) "Bild" the trail continues without much elevation change to the glacier."[lxxxvii]

As Ötzi trudged through the Tisenjoch pass, he entered on to the Giogo di Tisa Ridge. He walked around and looked out on to the Schnalsta Valley di Senales. But after the uphill hike, he stopped to rest and eat some meat (jerky). Hop hornbeam tree pollen grain from his gut indicated Otzi probably died in late spring, because that is when that tree blooms. This is in line with the season he would have started his journey. The tribal elders would have wanted the whole summer to relocate. Scientists have discovered his last meal was eaten no more than two hours before his death. This puts the time of his death in the early to mid-afternoon time frame. His full stomach shows he was not on the run.

During this refreshment, he had to make a decision. Should he take the trail down toward todays Similaun Hütte and then continue on to the valley floor? Or, seeing a river valley on his right, should he try to hike around to a ridge to get a better view of it's suitability? Ötzi's decision made him imortal.

Death Clues

Hinweise auf Seinen Tod

Indizi della Morte

Ötzi was an important discovery because he was wearing nine pieces of clothing which furnished the world's first set of non-burial Neolithic period attire. Previously, the oldest clothes were dated from 1500 B.C. So the Iceman provided the first opportunity to analyze clothing construction from before 3000 B.C. Previously only small amounts of material this old had been discovered.

As concerns the mystery about how he died, consider the Evidential Details surrounding the:

Clothing Clues

McMoneagle - I see him wearing skins, primarily, although there also seems to be some kind of grasses that have been woven that he is wearing as well. I can't tell if it's some kind of a basket he carries over his shoulder, or if it is part of his clothing. It is carried low, whichever it is. Grasses are wild, probably a very early form of wheat or rye. He of course has eaten the tops and saved the bottoms for use as part of his clothing. Mostly, he either wove stuff out of grasses to wear, or used the leather and skins from his food production.

Belt: The Iceman's calf leather belt was torn off on both sides of the sewn-on pouch. The belt fragment was 50 cm (19.7 in) long. Here was found unusual evidence of a ripping and tearing of considerable force.

Hat: The Iceman's hat was found 70 centimeters (27.5 in) from his head. The still tied chinstrap was broken. There has never been an explanation why Ötzi would rip the strap and remove his hat at one of the highest, hence coldest, points on his journey.

Pouch: The pouch was discovered torn, ripped and in general disrepair. So had someone else done this? Why?

Shoes: One of his size five cow hide shoes was found in good condition, the other was ripped open with no sole. But why would Ötzi walk through the mountains on one bare foot. And where did he get cow hide? Why would Ötzi destroy one shoe when it was critical for warmth on Alpine snow and ice, particularly when it was considered of good quality? He went down to his left and used that foot to attempt to stop.

South Tyrol Museum of Archaeology – www. iceman.it

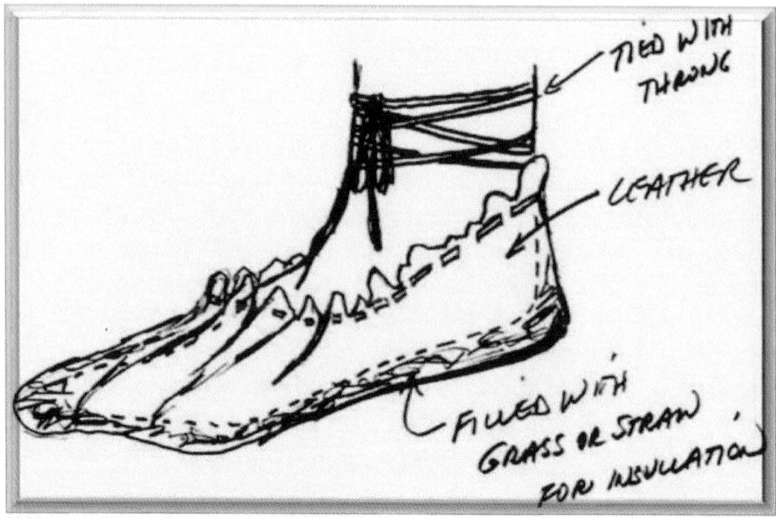

McMoneagle RV Art – Evidential Details ©1998

Ötzi's two left shoes, "*Filled with grass or straw for insulation.*" Here we observe the unknown way he tied his footwear. McMoneagle indicated the shoes were leather in 1998 even though scientists said they were bear skin. That was reversed to leather sometime in 2010.

Cape: With only 33% of his outer garment in-tact, something very dramatic had destroyed this outerwear. But why would anyone destroy warm clothing high in the Alps? Something had ripped it.

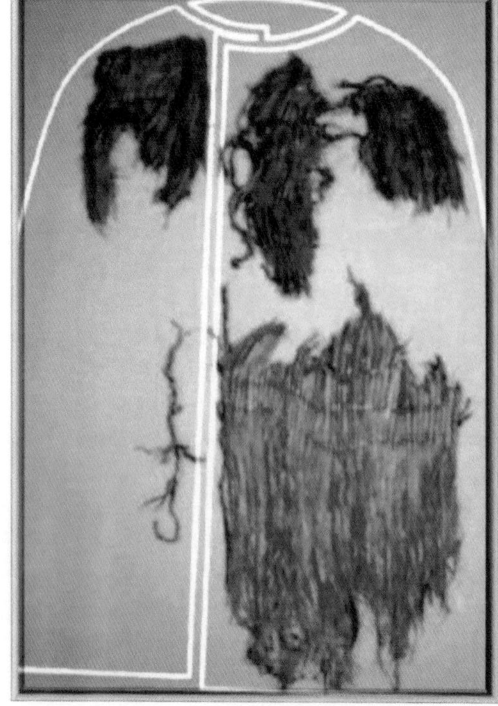

Ötzi's cape remains, made of gasses and long fibers from Linden Tree bark.

South Tyrol Museum of Archaeology – www. iceman.it

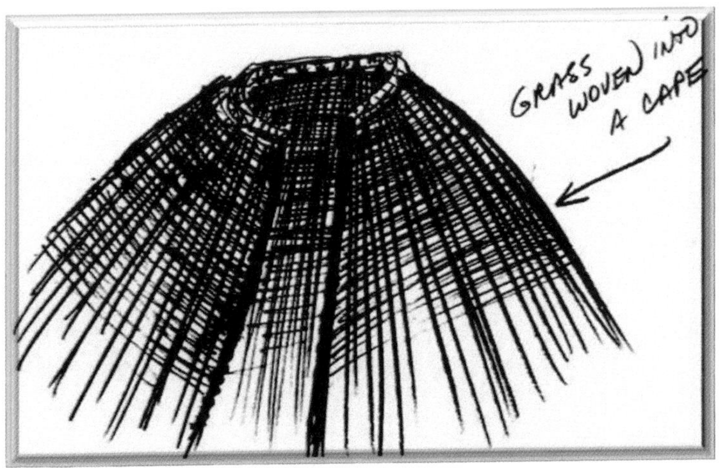

McMoneagle RV Art – Evidential Details ©1998
Pre-destruction appearance of the Iceman's cape.

His Flint and Pyrites: These items went missing when all the pieces of his pouch were spilled out.

His Back Pack: Made of hazel wood, the frame of his back pannier was broken into four pieces. Clearly, it would be foolish for the Iceman to break his backpack support. Who then took the time to smash the support rather than take this item for themselves?

In 1992, a 22+ centimeter (8.7in) broken bow stave end was discovered when the Ötzi site was re-examined. And three years after the mummy's recovery, the Head of the Osteological Research Laboratory at the University of Stockholm, Mr. Sojvold, found an overlooked piece of the Iceman's birch bark container five by eight inches (12.7 x 20.3cm) across.

Tool Clues

So, are there any Evidential Details in the tools that can help anthropologists understand why he died at this location?

McMoneagle – I see a bow, which is rather primitive, as well as some sharpened sticks in a kind of quiver. He is also carrying a longer stick or pole, which has a fire hardened point. I don't see any kind of flint at the end, so I suspect that he is living in an area which is predominantly small game (perhaps animals as large as a deer). He carries a small satchel made of skins, which contain flints, some bits of stone, and some kind of dyes.

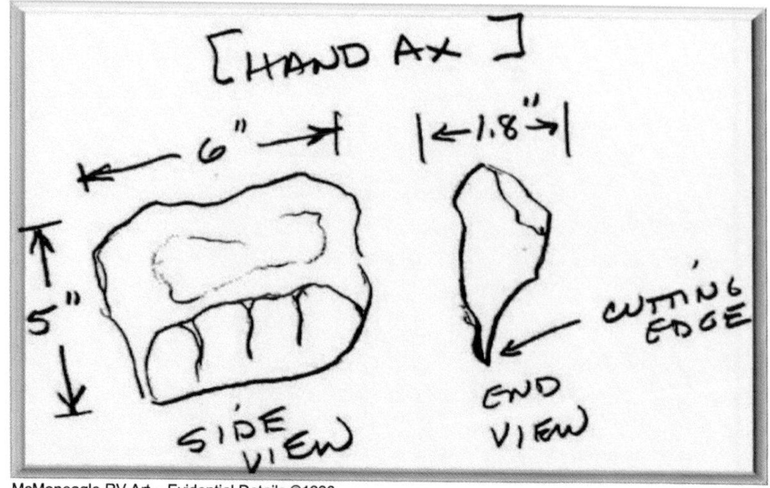

McMoneagle RV Art – Evidential Details ©1998

A missing artifact – Ötzi's unrecovered cleaving stone was 15.24cm wide x 12.7cm tall x 4.6cm thick

McMoneagle - Unrecovered artifact - You could conceivably say that a large flint stone with a cutting edge was a form of ax but there was no handle for it. It was only carried in his satchel which was woven from grass. I think it might be used for smashing bones and cleaving the game after it was dead.

It is possible this tool was also overlooked, as 5,300 years later it would have easily blended with surrounding rocks. Even more likely is that it was launched outward and is not at the site.

Birch Bark Container: The birch bark container lids, and all its contents, were missing. But, under what circumstance would the Iceman decide to rip the lid off and dump everything out? One theory maintained Ötzi was ambushed, ransacked, killed, carried up the mountain and then positioned into the trench!

Rope: The largest of the rope segments was 87cm (34 in) long and ripped at both ends. Clearly, hiking through the Alps meant the Iceman would want to have a rope at maximum length for mountaineering.

Ibex Horn: The ibex horn was well away from the body. Scientists have pondered why he removed it from its carrying case, set it on the ground, and then laid down to die elsewhere.

Fruit: Outside of its carrying case, scientists recovered a blackthorn fruit (*Prunus Spinosa*) also known as a sloe.

McMoneagle - I think he had a flint cutting tool, probably palm size. He also had a flint knife, but not with a handle, more of a blade, which he could cut through meat with. He also carried an awl like tool, which was made from bone, and sinew for repairing his clothing. Mostly he either wove stuff out of grasses to wear or used the leather and skins from his food production.

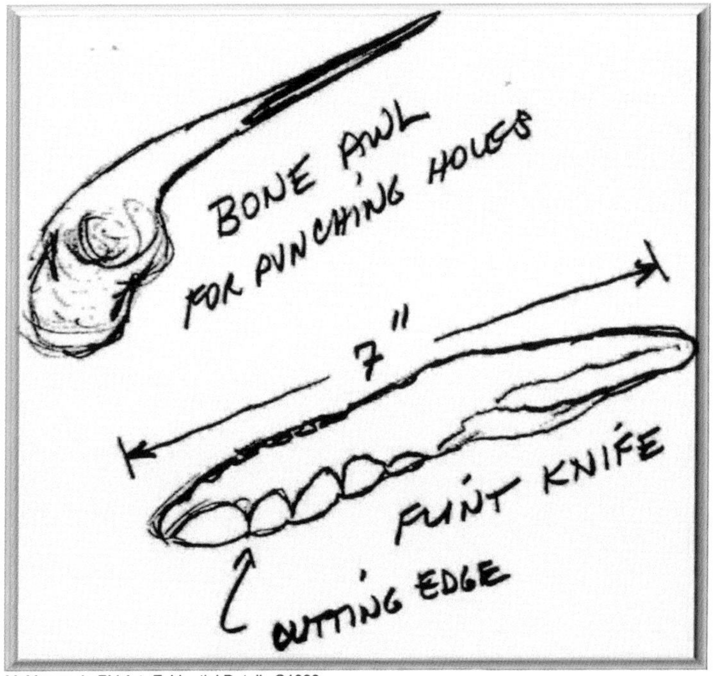

McMoneagle RV Art- Evidential Details ©1998

The "**bone awl for punching holes**" appears to be a combination of two tools. The flint knife McMoneagle referred to as "palm size" was correctly drawn but turned out to be seven centimeters (2.76in), not seven inches.

Copper Axe: The copper ax had a torn leather binding strip that had started to unwind. The unanswered question: why was something as critical as an axe allowed to fall into disrepair on an exploration this arduous?

Copper Axe Head Dagger

Dagger: The point of the flint dagger was broken and its scabbard damaged. The stone is reputed to be from Lake Garda, Italy. This leads some to believe this is where Ötzi originated. But these weapons were routinely bartered, stolen or removed from the dead. The handle (hilt) was made of ash. But, with unfinished bow and arrows, this now critical tool's broken tip made no sense.

Quiver: With this piece, researchers were able to confirm quivers were in use this early in man's evolution. While it is the oldest one in the world, they found the flap had been torn off and was nowhere near the quiver. Plus, the strap was missing. Oddly, the quiver was found 5 meters (16.4 feet) away from the body.

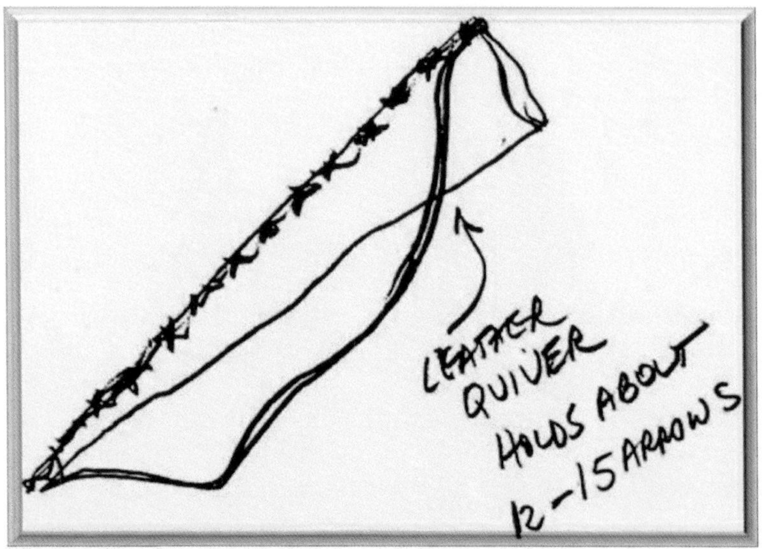

McMoneagle RV Art- Evidential Details ©1998 above and below.

McMoneagle clearly viewed the accoutrements on Ötzi's back. Here we see the world's oldest pre-destruction quiver. It is believed to have contained 12 arrows between 84 and 87cm long with one shorter than the rest.

Arrows: The quiver showed the arrow shafts were in good condition, but the two finished arrows were broken - one in two places. In addition, one flint arrowhead was broken with part of that arrowhead loose in the quiver. "The nature of the break suggests a high-energy impact; they had not just been stepped on...."[lxxxviii]

But it does not make sense that he broke his only functional arrows leaving none for hunting or self-defense while alone above the tree line, with a bad axe and a broken dagger.

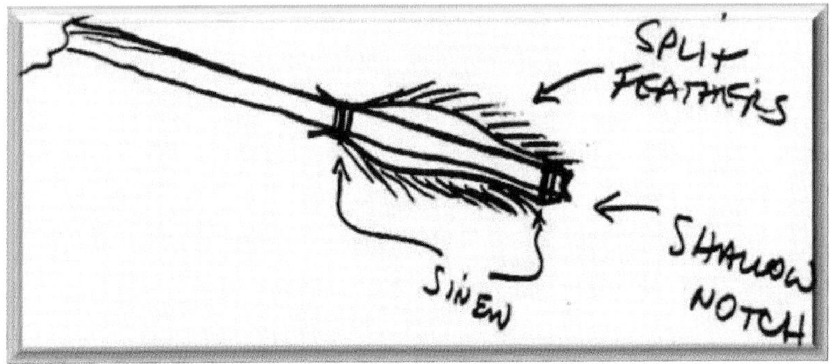

Our research showed Ötzi actually had three finished arrows made of viburnum sapwood. The others were unsmoothed. Once finished, the 1.82m/71.65 inch longbow could generate a force of 20 to 40 kilos (44 - 88 lbs.), with a skilled bowmen's "lethal" 90 meters (295 feet) outer range, and a maximum lobbing arc of 180 meters (590 feet). It was much more powerful than the unrecovered 41 inch Mesolithic bow Ötzi had used his whole life.

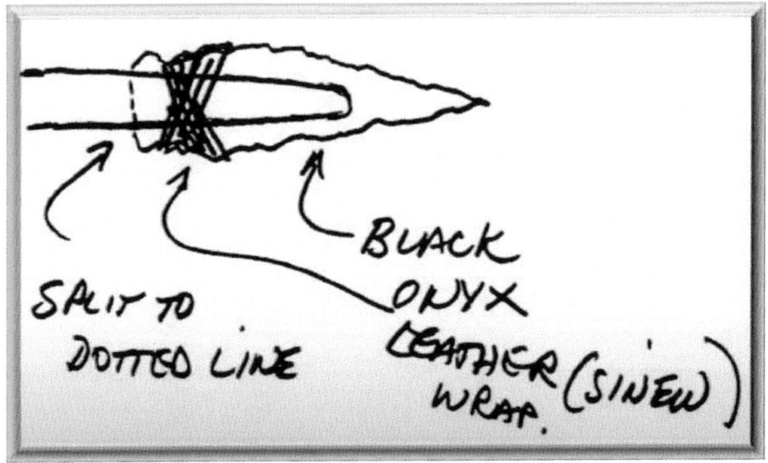

McMoneagle RV Art- Evidential Details ©1998

Lower picture - **McMoneagle:** (the shaft) **Split to Dotted Line; Black Onyx; Leather (Sinew) Wrap.** We believe Ötzi had three arrowhead tipped shafts. Someone else had made one of them which may have been bartered or found.

Bow(s): In the trench, his 1.83m (71.6 inch) unfinished bow was found without a bowstring. Made of yew (*Taxus baccata*), it was oddly fractured. It was found standing in an upright position, leading researchers to conclude it was deliberately placed there.

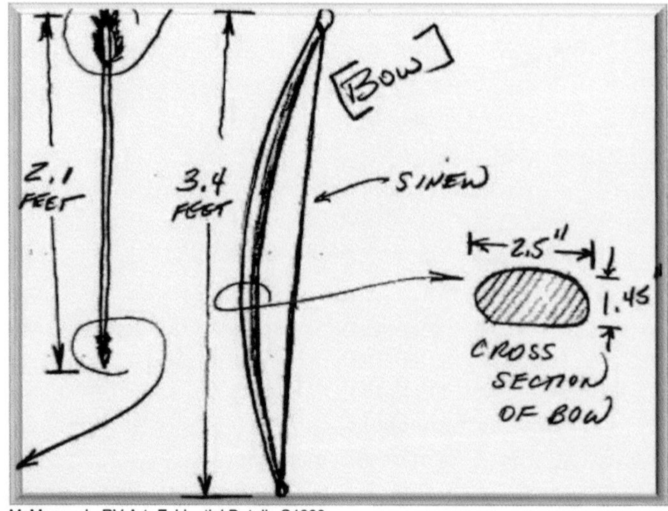

McMoneagle RV Art- Evidential Details ©1998

Previously unknown. Ötzi had two bows – his unrecovered 41-inch Mesolithic model (above) and the recovered, unfinished, Neolithic long bow. A 6.35cm by 3.7cm diameter, his Mesolithic bow was 1.04 meters. The arrows were 64cm long.

Overlooked by researchers is how Ötzi could kill swift hoofed mountain animals without a working bow. Given his mission, Ötzi certainly needed his Mesolithic bow while completing his unstrung long bow. He had carried his latest Neolithic project with him.

When told that, except for the cleaving stone and the smaller bow, these artifacts had all been recovered he said:

McMoneagle - Oh thanks a lot. Do you know how long it took me to draw those things?

With the scenarios of Ötzi being on the run, exploring, shepherding or ambushed, nobody knew the whys and wherefores of his final moments. So, approaching this as a crime scene, were there any evidential details on his body? Could Ötzi's wounds help solve this mystery?

Wound Clues

Scientists: "Because glacial ice moves and therefore slowly and relentlessly destroys anything in its path, the body required protection from glacial motion. The iceman was found frozen in ice in a natural trench oriented transverse to the glacial flow. Thus, while the body lay frozen in the ice-filled trench, the glacier passed over the iceman and left the corpse undisturbed." [lxxxix]

McMoneagle - And the way he died is very violent. I get a sense that he took a major blow to the head and possibly broke some other bones as well.

His Rib Cage

Human beings are possessed 12 ribs which are designated with a capital letter followed by the rib bone number. "In Ötzi's case, only 11 rib-bearing vertebrae were present. T (thorasic) 12 was lumbarized."[xc] But Ötzi's ribs were not just broken, they were oddly "*out of position.*"

Spindler: "*Here the X-ray shows that the third, fourth, fifth, and sixth ribs are broken and are somewhat out of position. In this case there is no callus formation, no trace of the bones having healed...*"[xci]

The two sides of Ötzi's rib cage were discovered as being asymmetrical. Doctors indicate ribs, like any other bone, start the healing process immediately after an initial blood and shock impact. They must be promptly attended to in order to set correctly. But Ötzi's ribs had not attempted to re-heal. Moreover, ribs, with no microscopic callus formation, could not have been broken for even an hour. But what was stranger, "The upper right part of the rib cage was strangely deformed, as if it had been smashed in from the top of the shoulder."[xcii] For some reason the top of Ötzi's rib cage had been crushed in with a major downward blow breaking his collar bone and shoulder. And his rib cage spinal connections were twisted and collapsed.

Scientists: "The thoracic deformity combines caudal rib rotation, rib subluxation (partial rib dislocation) at the costo-transverse and costo-vertebral (rib cartilages and vertebra) joints, and compression of the thorax. This combination suggests a balance of forces sufficient to cause these deformities."[xciii] "We attributed the combined features of rib rotation and thoracic compression to a **single dominant mechanism**."[xciv] With this, the PhDs and MD's should have quickly ruled out death by shoulder blade puncture.

His Shoulder Blade/Scapula

It was not until June 2001, that an arrowhead was discovered in Ötzi's shoulder blade. This area was not examined through multi-slice tomography until August of 2005.

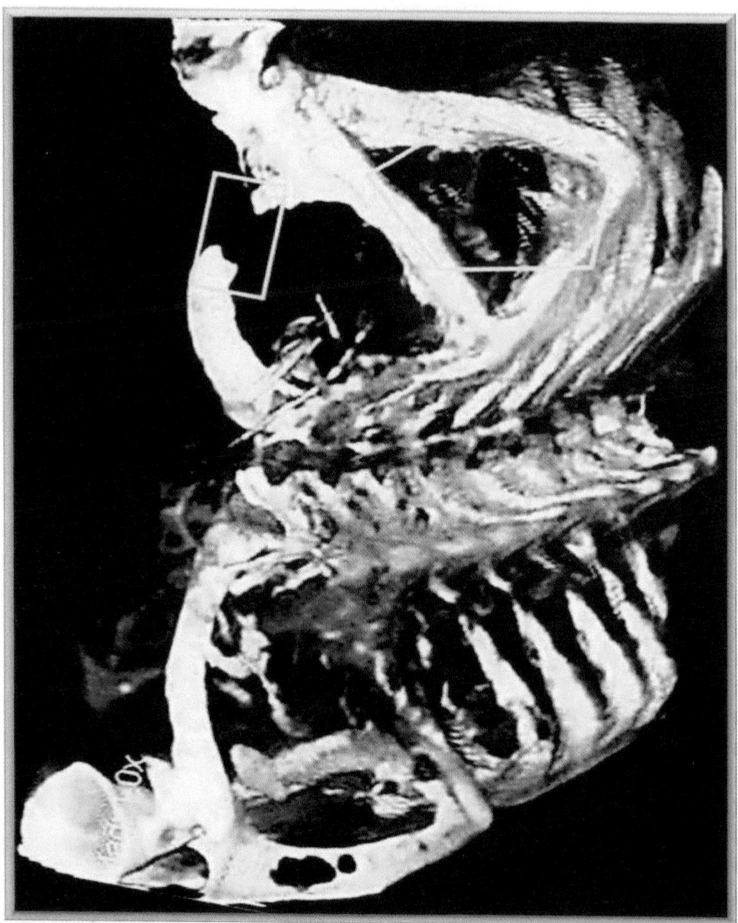

M.D. Anderson Radiological

A CT scan of Ötzi's spine showing the arrow head (center left) pointing upward without an attached arrow shaft (turn sideways). The top yellow rectangle shows the collar bone separation. The larger yellow box highlights the spatial differences between the rib cage's left and right side. The left side shows natural bone formation, and the right side shows the compression impact that came down through the collar bone. His torso was upside down during the "violent activity" that befell him.

Scientists: "One CT image (Computerized Tomography) showed what appeared to be evidence of penetration of the ossified (bone) body of the scapula (shoulder blade). In this location, the mineralized scapula was discontinuous. A small portion of the deep hematoma (blood pool) seemed to pass through the bone discontinuity. These findings were interpreted as evidence that the arrow passed through the scapula and injured a major vessel in the axilla (arm pit), with a resultant hematoma."

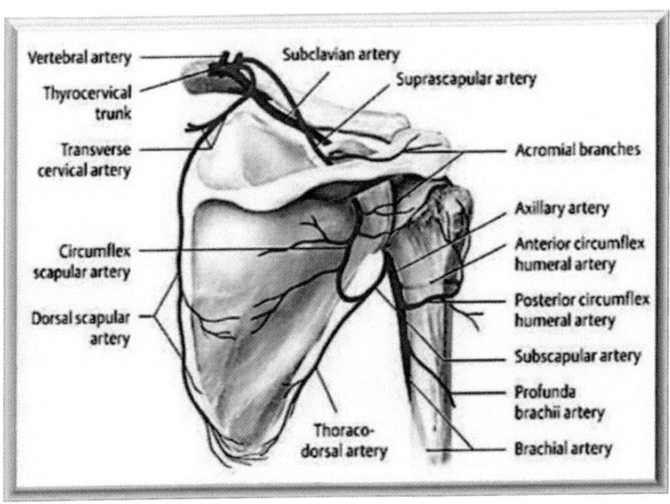

"When the iceman was found frozen in the glacier, there was no arrow protruding. Inspection of his back following discovery of the arrowhead in June 2001 revealed a small skin laceration over the scapula, close to the region where the discontinuity was present in the scapula. It was hypothesized that an arrow entered the iceman's left shoulder from the rear and caused a vascular injury. Furthermore, it is speculated that when the arrow was withdrawn, the overlying scapula interfered and caused the arrowhead to separate from the shaft. Thus, the arrowhead remained trapped between the rib cage and the scapula."

"On the basis of discovery of the arrowhead and correlation with a tract, verified with a probe, the cause of the iceman's death appears to be bleeding secondary to a puncture wound caused by an arrow. The manner of death, based on the location of the arrowhead and the fact that it entered from the rear, can be classified as either accidental or homicide. All of these image-derived findings and hypotheses remain to be corroborated in other future investigations."[xcv] It was all wrong. There was no death from a one inch arrowhead.

McMoneagle - He could have just as easily fell (fallen) **on his own arrows as well. Usually, it is quite clear when someone has been shot with an arrow. It hits bones going in and leaves a very identifiable mark. I'm surprised they didn't find this/these marks a lot sooner, especially since he was bodily intact.**

From the CT scan, the arrowhead's entrance angle implies Ötzi was shot when bent forward or, upward by someone kneeling below him. All this confirms Ötzi wore his quiver slung toward his left shoulder and that the arrowhead was forced in by some powerful action. Curiously, there was no arrow shaft exit wound.

We reviewed these assertions with an Orthopedic Surgeon and a Registered Nurse who was also an archery instructor. She agreed with the cardio-braccia artery theory which is nestled in the armpit (axilla). But physicians recognize such a wound is not immediately mortal and death would have taken days due to the arrowhead's small size. Doctors realize an arrowhead of 1 inch by .7 inch (2.5 x 1.8cm) in the shoulder blade will not immediately kill an adult. And with no callus formation in the rib joints, the whole arrow shot to the shoulder blade scenario was never a plausible cause of death so immediate as to block all calcium formation. Additionally:

"The arrowhead need not have caused death. Many people stay alive after foreign objects such as bullets have entered their bodies. A notable archaeological example is the Cascade spear point in the right pelvis of the famous Kennewick Man in North America; it had been there long enough for the bone to begin healing around it. Even more recently, in a statement to the media, Egarter Vigl has reported that Ötzi's right hand reveals a deep stab wound. No scientific publication of this finding has been made yet."[xcvi]

The hand stab wound alleged as a defensive combat wound was actually a protective move from a swift fall against jagged rock. Scientists determined it to be less than 18 hours old. It was less than 18 minutes old.

Slowly bleeding to death allows for some healing calcification in broken bones. It is clear Ötzi did not bleed to death because there was no healing. Theories that require a lapse in time to heal may be confidently discarded.

His Telltale Legs

From the scientific reports of 2000 and 2008, we found separate scientific examinations that came to the same conclusion about Ötzi's non-Neolithic legs.

Scientists: "The anterior tubercles of the tibiae were wide, thick, and prominent.[15] The thick lower-extremity long-bone cortices, prominent nutrient canals, exaggerated anteroposterior (front to rear bone) diameters, and conspicuous linea asperae[16] and tibial tubercles suggested presence of powerful lower-extremity musculature. Unfortunately, the profound dehydration obscured the actual original muscle bulk."[xcvii]

Scientists: "His femur[17] is about average in strength compared to our late Neolithic...males, but his tibia is well above average. His femur also shows adaptations for his relatively broad body (mediolateral strengthening),[18] while his tibia shows adaptations for high mobility over rough terrain (anteroposterior strengthening).[19] In many respects, his tibia more closely resembles those of European Mesolithic rather than Neolithic males, which may reflect a more mobile lifestyle than was characteristic of most Neolithic males, perhaps related (or unrelated) to a pastoral subsistence strategy."[xcviii] Making the Mesolithic point again, "Second, the tibiae and fibulae[20] exhibited exaggerated anteroposterior diameters.

These femoral, tibial, and fibular diaphyseal (long bone shaft) shapes appear to reflect the mechanical force or loading placed on them during lifetime activity." "It is surmised that this configurational oddity indicates a bio-mechanical adaptation to the requirements of life and labor on the slopes of the Alps."[xcix] But, this is only an "oddity" if you go into the lab with a predisposition.

Scientists: "Of interest were the conformational alterations of the lower-extremity long bones. First, the cortical (outer layer) thickness of the long bones was greater than that usually encountered in the average modern clinical population. It is speculated that constant climbing and hiking through the Alps would be sufficient to cause such muscle and bone development."[c]

From different scientific researchers we found mention of non-Neolithic leg bone structures more common to Mesolithic populations. These studies verified Ötzi was not originally from a Neolithic community. Scientists confirmed his non-Neolithic legs, but apparently no one, except Dr. Klaus Hollemeyer in 2008, has

---

15 A small rounded elevation on the bone.
16 A longitudinal ridge in the middle third of the femur's posterior surface.
17 Femur - The strongest bone in the human skeleton, the thigh bone that extends from the hip to the knee.
18 Bone strength passing through the femur from the middle to the side. (radius)
19 Bone strength passing through the femur from front to rear. (diameter)
20 Fibulae (plural) The outer and smaller leg bone between the ankle and the knee.

been quoted on it as of this writting:

"*There is a long lasting debate about the socio-cultural state of Iceman's society,*" lead researcher Klaus Hollemeyer of Saarland University in Germany told Live Science. "*One faction says he belongs to the gatherer-hunter society, which is more primitive than the more progressive pastoral-agricultural society which followed after.*"[ci]

Our data explained this question ten years (1998) before Professor Hollemeyer took this interview question.

His Skull/Cranium

The skull was found with deformities. A suture is the line of union between two bones in the skull. The lambdoid suture is between the occipital and two parietal bones. Ötzi's skull had been fractured. But scientists said his brain had also been "fractured."

Scientists: "When scrutinized more closely, the CT images showed the presence of numerous hair-line fractures or cracks of the facial bones and the base of the skull. These were associated with slight widening of sutures in particular, the lambdoid suture." [cii]

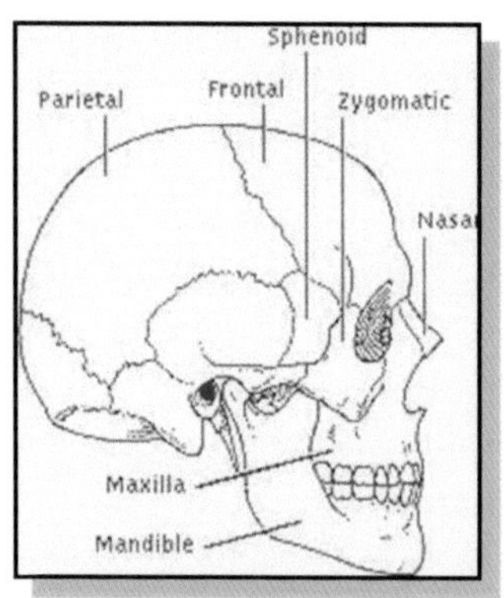

The Zygomatic Bone - "A small bone in vertebrates on each side of the face socket, forming the prominence of the cheek, also called cheek bone."[ciii] Also, his fractured nose, shown as Nasal (middle right), was flattened from the bridge down - an unusual wound as most nose fractures are upward or sideways.

Spindler: There exists, "*...a fracture of the right zygomatic arch with a displacement of the fracture faces by just over 2 milli-metres. The right boney eye socket is also slightly sheered.*" (sheared)[civ]

Scientists: "The tip of the nasal bone was fractured, and the fragment was angled approximately 90° downward. This fracture was different from the other skull fractures because it was on the surface of the face in an exposed location and because it manifested considerable angulation. If the fracture was acquired from an injury during life, as from a direct blow, it shows no evidence of healing."[cv] Immediate healing arrest.

Scientists: "Transverse CT images showed multiple unhealed facial cracks and fractures. Stereo-lithographic reproduction demonstrated recession of the face with slightly greater displacement on the left side compared with the right side. The skull and facial bones were characterized mathematically, and results confirmed recession of the midface and base of the skull."[cvi]

This is consistent with our conclusions. Ötzi's face was smashed downward just before his death. It had not started to heal in the few moments before he passed away.

Scientists: "Skeletal variants were present, as was evidence of degenerative arthritis, frostbite, vascular calcification…"[cvii]

Postmortem

The totality of the ripped clothing, injuries, ripped clothing with broken and scattered tools developed into a bizarre pattern of extreme violence. The question remained, for what purpose would Ötzi place his quiver 16 feet (4.87m) away from where he died? Why would his most important equipment be spread out? With the arrow shot idea, researchers have conveniently attributed these key details to Ötzi's purported unusual behavior, Neolithic crime scene mayhem, or excavation errors!

Scientists: "Our imaging findings correlate well with the gross findings of desiccation (drying), with little evidence of putrefaction (decomposition) or adipocere formation, also known as grave wax. The dominant form of postmortem change found in most glacial human remains is adipocere, and glacial bodies tend to be diffusely infiltrated by this substance.[21] As opposed to this common situation, the iceman had no visible adipocere."[cviii]

No putrefaction, or odor, or callus formation, confirms Ötzi was frozen quickly. But, the caving in of his ribs would appear as a different wound than if post death, and most PhD theories are in the face of no putrefaction.

Others have asserted, "The (small) stone arrowhead was found in Ötzi's left shoulder was thought to have caused the pre-

---

[21] Adiopocere - wax like substance composed of fatty acids and calcium soaps associated with bodily decay.

historic man's death, fatally severing his left subclavian artery."[cix] But this leads to a slow death allowing callous formation. It has always been apparent that, given the speed of his molecular arrest, a slow death is impossible. The shoulder wound, as an explanation of the cause of death, remains medically unworkable.

Other death scenarios include that the Iceman died at night as heavy weather came upon him, or, that he was attempting to escape when his town was attacked.

But Ötzi researcher James Dickson, an expert in botanical archaeology and paleoecology at the Scottish University of Glasgow said: *"Our knowledge of the events immediately before* (Ötzi's) *death ... is poor."*[cx]

Spindler: "*Time and again during our research we have been compelled to adjust our views... The uniqueness of the discovery makes unprecedented demands on the scientists involved.*"[cxi]

Scientists: "Without other evidence, we will not be able to determine more about the circumstances surrounding the Iceman's death."[cxii]

And according to an American Scientific article:

"But we do not know and may never know what reason Ötzi had for being at a great altitude in the Alps. And we may never understand exactly how he died."[cxiii]

Death Mystery Solved

"The Single Dominant Mechanism"

Das Todes Rätsel ist Gelöst

"Die Einzigen Dominierenden Mechanismus"

Morte Mistero Risolto

"Il Singolo Meccanismo Dominante"

In his last 36 hours, Ötzi hiked through different habitats enroute south from Vent. He entered the Niederjoch, which is the north/south watershed connective yoke (joch). In what remains the most plausible scenario, Ötzi arrived around midday. He went to the ridge and viewed the pre-lake Val Senales River Valley.

Jakob Tappeiner

The Austro-Italian border looking north as the sun sets. Ötzi moved (**orange line**) sideways off the path to get to the mountain spine (**yellow line**) but never made it.

Tired from the uphill morning hike, he sat down to eat and rest while deciding what to do as he looked out at the cold but beautiful view. For that day's second meal, he ate red deer meat (*Cervus Eelaphus*) in a fan moss wrap (Neckera Complanata).[22]

The evidence that Ötzi ate an hour or two before his death adds up. He was relaxing on a full belly – not on the run. So, should he continue along the path, or should he get a closer look at the river valley off to his right? Archaeologists have always wondered why Ötzi was found in a gully away from the main path. He decided to explore out on to the mountain ridge. We concluded he was trying to get to a Val Senales River Valley over-look to check for inhabitants without actually encountering them.

---

[22] Other reports say he had ibex meat in his stomach. He may have had both. Ötzi had 36 samples of six different mosses in five intestinal areas.

With rising interest, Ötzi moved westward toward the Rabenspitz (3265m/10,712ft) mountainside spine. Once he got onto it he would have passed a point known as the Gran Cadola (2972m/9,750ft) on his way down to the end-point called alternately Drei Wärter/Le Tre Guardie/The Three Guardsmen, (2732m /8,963ft). If no one was there, Otzi might be able to return triumphant in his explorations thereby re-establishing his tribal worth.

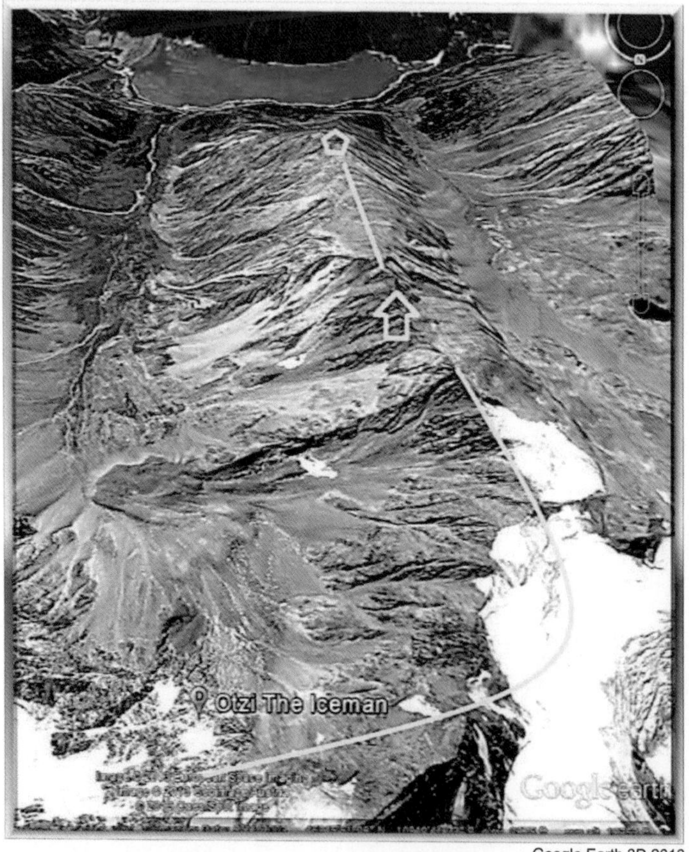

Google Earth 3D 2013

Reverse angle viewing the modern **Lake Vernago** river valley overlook. Given his task, Ötzi was skirting the mountain to explore the valley via this mountain spine. From this vantage point, (**yellow base top**), he could see if there was any camp fire smoke along the river before hiking down. This would have been a 542m/1,775ft downhill hike. The **maroon marker** (lower left) is where Ötzi was found.

McMoneagle - Mr. 'Ugly' was off on a journey to seek out and find a new area that they might move to for new game. It is getting harder and harder to find game where they cur-

rently reside. He is about eight days into his journey and trying to negotiate a very difficult passage through a place in the mountains. I get a great sense of a place, which is filled with ice and snow, exposed rocks, wind, and it is not very pleasant. ...he was traversing the side of a mountain crossing ...its southern or west-southwest side.

McMoneagle RV Art - Evidential Details ©1998

The eyeball sketch as Ötzi was weaving his way sideways along the mountain. As he moved into a precarious place, he would have been watching his step as he looked thousands of feet down.

He is trying to move along the edge of a ledge and essentially the ledge just gives out, causing him to fall to his death. He tumbles and slides and strikes his head hard against stones (at) **the bottom of a ravine or cut in the mountain. His fall is approximately 80 to 90 yards. I don't think he ever regained consciousness, but probably went into a coma and died from exposure.**

Ötzi's fall appears to be 92 meters, which is 303 feet at 46°46'45.8N – 10°50'25.1E. Plunging down the steep rough grade, he slammed against jagged rock outcroppings, flipping and tumbling. Falling at up to 160 mph (257kph) at some points, he hit upside-down smashing his nose and collarbone downward creating an upside down serial rib fracture with spinal dislocation.

Google Earth 2021

Ötzi moved off the path (top right) attempting to skirt the mountain attempt to scout the valley (left side) He started from the Giogo di Tisa ridge moving left to get to the Gran Cadola. He fell about 23 stories into the Tisenjoch Saddle (red dot center).The historian can now better assess the fugitive crime scene arrow shot theory.

Shotview

Otzi fell into the 8' deep trench along the **red dots**, hitting his head face up on the rock that stopped his fall. He rolled over onto his arm and went into a coma. His ax, bow and backpack hit the trench floor and bounced up onto the far side (lower left).

Summersaulting, his items spilled out of his pouch. Heavier, the cleaving stone went flying off in a wider trajectory. His rope, quiver, hat strap, leather belt, pouch, back pack and second birch bark container were all subjected to high speed ripping, tearing and grinding, against a sharp rock downward gravitational pull. Trying to stop, the base of his thumb was cut to the bone.

His larger Neolithic bow was partially broken. But his strung Mesolithic bow snapped and launched itself outside the trench. The quiver went up driving an arrow into his shoulder blade which was then immediately broken off. The dagger's tip was broken against mountain rock, and his equipment spread out as it bounced up on to the trench's far side. His hat flew when he hit his head on stone at free fall speed ripping the chin strap.

"The finding spot of the mummy is located in a 40 m-long, (131ft) 2.5 m-deep (8ft) and 5 to 8 m (16 to 26ft) wide rocky gully surrounded by steep stone walls 73 m (239.5ft) below the Giogo di Tisa ridge..."[cxiv] He was on the trench's west end. There was clearly no time for "*deadly hemorrhagic shock.*"

McMoneagle - I can't tell where this place is that he took this fall from, only that it was up in some mountains which have lots of snow on them. I get a sense that the snow is perpetual, in other words, it does not go away in the summer, so it is probably above ten thousand feet and in some kind of alpine area. It is either North America, or Europe. Given the age of this guy, I would opt for Europe.

How much time between the skull hitting stone to death? Not long. Scientists can reference this. But, his body has undoubtedly verified he did not bleed to death. The arrow to the shoulder blade could not have killed the Iceman quickly enough to stop all putrefaction and bone calcium formation. Since 1998, falling has remained the most believable scenario.

Ötzi landed hard on his back fracturing his skull/brain on the rock next to where he was found. He rolled off the stone onto his stomach with his left arm pinned underneath his chin - ear folded over - lip pushed up. In a coma, he was immediately frozen with no internal healing or putrefaction. A further examination found bruises and cuts to the hands, wrists and chest.

McMoneagle - My real-time sense of this guy is that he is dried out like hard leather. So, he must in some way have been mummified or smoked? Very dry. So, it is possible that

this place was either very cold at the time of his death, or he fell into a place which didn't have any water access to it. It was perhaps the entry to a small cave or cut in the rocks which quickly sealed itself off from the world with heavy snow. So, this was probably an area that was adjacent to or very close to a major glacier. Lots of blue ice. Old ice. It is very difficult to tell, because he is apparently somewhat mummified or smoked (preserved). Very hard to figure since this guy is probably very well preserved---still 'Ugly' as sin, but well preserved. Maybe he's so 'Ugly' the women threw him out of the tribe. (seriously!) There could be something to this.

Anton Koler

Ötzi emerges from the ice. This picture was taken from the upper right corner of the cover photo. His head hit the rock next to his left shoulder face up, "fracturing" his skull and brain.[cxv] With this brain injury (see broken skin on his skull), he went into a coma and was immediately frozen thereby arresting all molecular processes.

Scientists: "When the Iceman's mitochondrial DNA was analyzed by Franco Rollo and his colleagues, it was discovered that he had genetic markers associated with reduced fertility (reduced sperm count). It has been speculated that this may have affected his social acceptance or at least that his infertility could have had social implications within his tribal group..."[cxvi]

Scientists: "Dr. Rollo said, 'One would have to investigate whether there was an awareness of male infertility in this ancient society; and if so, whether the lack of a family or clan could represent a kind of social weakness.'"[cxvii]

If it is true that Ötzi was a reproductive outcast, it could be why he journeyed to the Remedello village. Analysis also showed him at high risk of atherosclerosis, lactose intolerance, and that he is the earliest known human being studied with Lyme disease.

Another reason Ötzi may not have been welcome would have been due to his absence in the Remedello community. Without children, he was not hunting for the tribe. His failure to bring food to those in the serious business of keeping children alive may have emerged with "*you're not a contributor*" disdain.

When the human body becomes sick and fights infection, fingernails stop growing. Once they start again, Beau's lines form across the nail revealing where the growth stoppage occurred.

Years after these remote viewing sessions, scientists released Ötzi's fingernail data. It showed that three Beau's lines were discovered across his nails indicating he had been stricken with illness three times in the last six months. I went back to McMoneagle.

Follow-up Question: "I learned that recently the fingernails of the Iceman were analyzed and it seems that nail growth is somewhat like tree rings. Growth rates can be determined as normal, or retarded due to sickness, when the body marshal's its energies away from nail growth to fight disease. The Iceman showed retarded nail growth before he departed upon his journey. Then I remembered something you said about the women disrespecting this guy. I wonder if this was due to being sickly for a while. If so, it would add up that this tribe elder could be mocked by younger women because he was older and needed support to get through his sickness. My understanding is that non-productive tribal members were not respected. Any thoughts on this?

McMoneagle - I think in his time period, there probably wasn't so much disrespect for the sick or elderly, as there was indifference. They didn't know what sickness was in the elderly, as it wouldn't fit the same scenario that they would understand for young virile people - like wounds, infections, that sort of thing.

If someone started having a heart problem for instance - shortness of breath, inability to labor, they would simply look on it as laziness or inability to perform necessary

tasks for survival. The tendency would be to just ignore them till they died or walked off never to be seen again. I think that's essentially what he did probably, in the hopes of proving his worth perhaps by finding better hunting...

A New Scenario

Ein Neues Szenario

Un Nuovo Scenario

Among the items that distinguish the Neolithic from the Mesolithic epoch are polished rather than chipped tools, foundry, pottery, expanded naturopathy and the nutrition available from an agro-economy that included multi-animal husbandry. In addition, emerging specializations like weapons, cobblery and clothes construction were available for barter in a Neolithic village as large as in the Val Venosta Valley. It is here that Mr. McMoneagle shines a light on this historically obscure transition.

Ötzi originated from a small Mesolithic tribe centuries into the Neolithic period. Their way of life was on the defensive in the face of increasing expansion around the Alpine lakes and rivers.

Spindler: "*The real opening up of the Alps took place in the Late Neolithic, which probably started no later than about 4000 B.C. The first extensive forest clearances were carried out in the valley landscapes favouring settlement, and new forms of agriculture were developed specifically for the high mountains.*"[cxviii]

"From now on there was a great deal of movement in Europe. Various cultural groups went from place to place, sometimes to settle there, sometimes to stay only a few generations and then go on." "The first Neolithic idea-bearing people arrived in regions that were already inhabited. Since there are no written records we cannot be certain how the old hunting and new farming cultures mixed, but the physical remains of the time seem to indicate that the newcomers did not meet much resistance."[cxix]

"Perhaps the most important development in Neolithic times was the drawing together of people into larger social units. The hunters had lived their more or less nomadic existence in small bands: now with a more settled economy, villages and towns became possible."[cxx] And, "villagers and farmers, men and women lived longer than they did as hunters."[cxxi] In Europe "The days of the free-roaming but always insecure nomad were passing."[cxxii]

Pathologist's observations confirm the Iceman's remains belonged to a hunter-gather existence. Mr. McMoneagle refers to the Iceman's awareness of shepherding and milking, but that his tribe did not participate. Nor did they have an alchemic capability which is industry's base. Without livestock, they cooked with unpolished implements in shells. Their language skills were likely viewed as behind the curve. Now, their hunting range was not only being reduced, it was dangerous.

As Neolithic populations grew, deforestation resulted in diminished hunting ranges. "With the 'hoe culture' a square mile of territory can support three people, three times the number per square mile in a hunting and gathering economy. With full agriculture (plowing), a square mile of arable land will support 750 persons, thus allowing for a tremendous increase in population."[cxxiii]

Standing on the Endekopt mountain (2,627m/8,618 feet), Ötzi had a panoramic valley view north of Lake Haidersee. Here he could see row housing, livestock, sheparding and milking. Through the seasons there were people planting, tending, and harvesting fields puncutated with the smoke of ancient smelting furnances.

With increasing health and longevity, the Lake Haidersee population expanded and further reduced the animal habitat. With slash and burn farming, wildlife would have fled into the Langtaufers Valley. It was a wonderfully long basin where people could drag game down a gentle slope or even float it out on the Karli Brook to the Adige River and south to the lake population. Langtaufers afforded Remedello tribesmen the opportunity to avoid mountain climbing.

In their time, the Langtaufers Valley was a great forested hunting ground except for one problem. There was a small Mesolithic tribe that would fight. Their tribe was considered dissimilar and unacceptable. Doctor, "Cavalli-Sforza's explanation of demic diffusions stipulated that the clines were due to the population expansion of Neolithic farmers into a scarcely populated, hunter-gathering Europe, with little initial admixture between agri-culturalists and foragers."[cxxiv] So, as the Remedello ventured up into Langtaufers, conflicts broke out over what was a great game habitat for animals seeking refuge from the deforested Val Venosta Valley floor now Lake Resia.

We concluded Ötzi's tribe was centered in Kappl, Italy, because the constant ambient sound of cascading waterfalls must have been an attractive place to establish a village. Plus, there was opportunity to hunt safely eastward toward the modern town of Melago and on into the mountains.

Scientists: "As the "Neolithic package" (including farming, herding, polished stone axes, timber longhouses and pottery) spread into Europe, the Mesolithic way of life was marginalized and eventually disappeared. Mesolithic adaptations such as sedentism, population size and use of plant foods are cited as evidence of the transition to agriculture. However in north-eastern Europe, the hunting and fishing lifestyle continued into the med-ieval period in regions less suited to agriculture."[cxxv]

Ötzi's tribe had retained a Mesolithic culture that, century after century, fell behind the curve. But even up to the nineteenth century's end, certain nomadic people were loath to give up this lifestyle. This is because, in part, "our memories of the chase linger in our joyful pursuit of anything weak or fugitive, and in the games of our children - even in the word game."[cxxvi]

With the advantage of extended range longbow striking distances, Remedello hunting parties pressed up the Langtaufers Valley and skirmishes broke out. As Remedello hunter/warrior numbers increased, the writing was on the wall. As their hunting range dwindled, Ötzi's tribal leaders decided the coming summer did not bode well for the tribe's future.

Ötzi's people were, in all probability, pushed out when he was a teen. In no more time than the next generation's adulthood, it was necessary to determine if uncontested forest existed beyond the eastern mountain ridge.

Ötzi's tribal elders may also have been aware that else-where in the Alps, conquered villages faced extermination as we know from the 34 body mass grave at places like Talhiem. Indeed, for all that is known, there could be a mass grave in the Langtaufers Valley.

With a view to the larger sociological picture, the Iceman provides modern man with a unique window into European Mesolithic dislodgement.

Next page looking south. The Austrian-Italian border is a white and black line. From the Langtaufers Valley (unseen right side), Ötzi followed the streams to Vent (yellow line). Encountering people, he went south to a path that led over the Kreuzspitze peak (**brown line**) down and around to Vent again (**red line**). Blocked, he turned south exploring streams up into the eastern mountain range (**blue lines**) before coming to the Similaun. He moved westward off the trail (orange line) to get a look at the Val Senales Valley (**tan line**). On the way, he fell to his death (**purple circle**).

Ötzi: He hath honored me of late,
and I have bought
Golden opinions from all sorts
of people,
Which would be worn now
in their newest gloss.

William Shakespeare - *Macbeth*

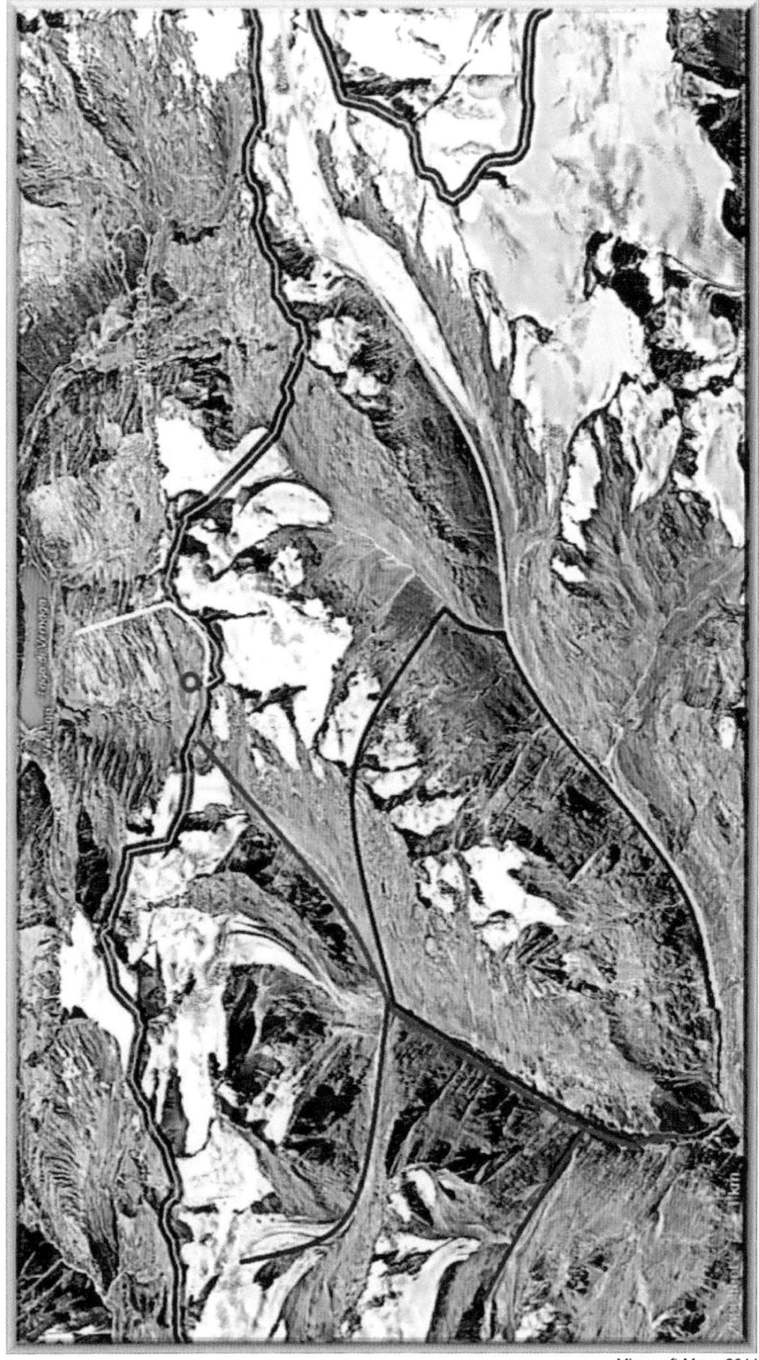

Microsoft Maps 2014

Afterword

Nachwort

Postfazione

Doctor Spindler's book had some humorous acknowledgements at the end including some of the frivolous names people have called the Iceman. So we thought our readers might also enjoy some humor. This Ötzi tasking was competed in 1998 before all the high technology scientific findings.

This book's first draft was submitted to some American publishers in 1999. The next year a book appeared with a paragraph about Ötzi's death that was unprecedented in the literature and without any scientific basis: About his death, it was written:

It was an accident to be sure. It looked like a bad fall, maybe through a precipice of snow that ...overhung the rocky shallow. ...this was the limit of his science.[cxxvii]

But speculating about a "precipice of snow" 5300 years later is not science. To write a year after our submission to the industry that Ötzi died, "*to be sure*" from a "*bad fall*" was unheard of. So what was the author's source? Under no conditions would we consider something as transient as a snowy precipice theory in any of the *Evidential Details Mystery Series*. When working with Controlled Remote Viewing, one needs to clarify time lines.

Many have wanted to be the one to determine Ötzi's death and there have been countless scenarios. The *Washington Post* reported the funniest by virtue of its being entitled "Case Closed" on a subject that will never be closed. The *Post* article read in part: "*A team of scientists in Italy has concluded that the 5,300-year-old Bronze Age hunter ...died from a wound from an arrow that ripped through his back.*"[cxxviii]

This article echoed the idea Ötzi died in a mountaintop execution! But, "*The angle of the wound suggests Ötzi's assailants fired from below*."[cxxix] Given the trench's position, below what?

Then there was the 2016 Public Broadcasting System's *Nova* program showcasing their very impressive Ötzi 3D printer replication. The show was designed to build credibility to support the Bolzano Museum's increasingly precarious arrow shot theory. University of Austria's Archaeological Department Chair, Dr. Leitner, was not in the credits. However, South Tyrol Museum's Director Dr. Fleckinger, and their picture sales lady were.

In their review *Nova* correctly acknowledged, "*His Culture was in transition*", that Ötzi was, "*Well suited for a hunter*", and that some ancient Europeans, "*still lived in pockets*." But, *Nova* failed to point out that scientists agree Ötzi's leg muscularization could not have come from farming.

Nova's bottom line was that "*occasional*" DNA mutations create nature's "*random mistakes*". That, "*Every once in a while you get a mutation, and that mutation, sometimes, ends up spreading*." Hair and eye chromosomes were swirling early on, but Otzi's "*Neolithic farmer*" DNA was not.

Entered into this mix was the extraordinary news of a large Turkish farmer migration into the Alp's that pushed the natives out. "*This wave of* (Turkish) *farmers that swept through Europe...*" supposedly affected Ötzi's genome. So naturally his ancestry came, "*...from the earlier farmer immigrants*." But what is a "*farmer genome*" and since when can genomes determine occupation?

Then *Nova* stated, "*His closest living* (DNA) *relatives were on the island of Sardinia*."[cxxx] With a whirling double helix, they failed to explain the connection between their Ötzal Alp Turkish cousins. And unknown to historians was their flat statement that in 3,300 B.C., all Sardinian's were farmers. So, an open and shut case was made for "*his closeness*" to a farmer genome! This is not the first time DNA has been used to perpetrate a business model.

As it turned out, the evidence (Evidential Details) pointed to Ötzi's transitioning from a Mesolith to a Neolith. His shining a light into this transitional period certainly makes him more valuable. We are sure Ötzi would be delighted to know of his modern celebrity. It is hoped this information will help the sciences generate the most accurate conclusions about the man the world has come to know and love as *Ötzi the Iceman*.

Ötzi: I have touched the highest point

of all my greatness,

And from that full meridian of my glory,

I haste now to my setting. I shall fall

Like a bright exhalation in the evening

And no man see me more.

William Shakespeare – *Henry VIII*

Ötzi Langtaufer

Transition Man

Bibliography

- Alpenwelt- Travel.com maps.
- Barnett, Lincoln and the Editors of *Life*; *The Epic of Man*; Golden Press, Inc. 1962
- Böhler, Günther; *Examining Magistrate Report*; September, 1991
- Burenhult, Goran, General Editor; *The Illustrated History of Human kind - The People of the Stone Age - Hunter-gatherers and Early Farmers*; Volume II; American Museum of Natural History; HarperSanFrancisco; 1993
- Dickson, James H, Oeggl, Klaus, Handley, Linda L.; Scientific American, *The Iceman Reconsidered*; 2003
- Durant, Will; *The Story of Civilization: Part I – Our Oriental Heritage*; Simon and Schuster, New York; 1954
- Egarter, Gostner P, Vigl E.; *Report of radiological-forensic findings on the Iceman*, Archaeological Science, 2002
- Fowler, Brenda; *Iceman*, Random House, 2000
- Heiss, Andreas G. and Oeggl, Klaus; *Abstract*; Institute of Botany, University of Innsbruck, Austria; Received: December 2006, Accepted: October 2007, Published online: January 2008
- Holzknect, Helmut, 1991 *Police Report* - City of Solden, Austria
- Ives, Sarah; *National Geographic News* article, 2003
- Jones, Tom B. *Ancient Civilization*, University of Minnesota, Rand McNally & Company, 1960
- Leitner, Dr. Walter, Institute for Archeology, University of Innsbruck; Pre- and Early History, and Medieval Archeology and Modern Times
- Lippert, A., Gostner, P., Egarter Vigl, E., Pernter, P., Vom Leben und Sterben des Ötztaler Gletschermannes. Germania 2007
- Lorenzi; Rossella, *Blow to head, not arrow, killed Ötzi the Iceman*; *Discovery News*, 2007
- Loy, Tom; *Blood on the Axe*; Center for Molecular and Cellular Biology, University of Queensland, Brisbane, Australia - New Scientist Magazine
- Mauro, Salzano Francisco; Federal University of Rio Grande do Sul, Porto Alegre, Brazil, 2002.
- McMoneagle, Joseph, *The Ultimate Time Machine*; Hampton Roads Press, 1998
- Morelle, Rebecca; *Infertility link in Iceman's DNA*; BBC News science
- Murphy, William A. Jr, MD, *The Iceman: Discovery and Imaging*; The Division of Diagnostic Imaging, University of Texas M.D. Anderson Cancer Center, Houston, TX 77030 From the 1994 RSNA scientific assembly. Received March 25, 2002; revision requested June 10; revision received July 26; accepted August 1.; with the Department of Radiology II, University of Innsbruck, Austria (D.z.N., W.R.); Department of Radiology, Regional General Hospital, Bolzano, Italy (P.G.);
- Nova National Geographic Special, *Iceman Murder Mystery* Copyright 2011, NGHT LLC, WGBH Educational Foundation

Part III

...as a result of my own previous exposure to this (remote viewing) community I became persuaded that war can almost always be traced to a failure in intelligence, and that therefore the strongest weapon for peace is good intelligence.

~ H. E. Puthoff, PhD. ~

Founder and First Director (1972-1985)
The Military Intelligence program known as Operation Star Gate

JOSEPH W. MCMONEAGLE, CW2, US Army, *Owner/Executive Director of Intuitive Intelligence Applications, Inc.*

Mr. McMoneagle has 34 years of professional expertise in research and development, in numerous multi-level technical systems, the paranormal, and the social sciences. Experience includes: experimental protocol design, collection and evaluation of statistical information, prototype design and testing, Automatic Data Processing equipment and technology interface, management, and data systems analysis for mainframe, mini-mainframe, and desktop computer systems supporting information collection and analysis for intelligence purposes.

He is currently owner and Executive Director of Intuitive Intelligence Applications, Inc., which has provided support to multiple research facilities and corporations with a full range of collection applications using Anomalous Cognition (AC) in the production of original and cutting edge information. He is a full time Research Associate with The Laboratories for Fundamental Research, Cognitive Sciences Laboratory, Palo Alto, California, where he has provided consulting support to research and development in remote viewing for 16+ years. As a consultant to SRI-International and Science Applications International Corporation, Inc. from 1984 through 1995, he participated in protocol design, statistical information collection, R&D evaluations, as well as thousands of remote viewing trials in support of both experimental research as well as active intelligence operations for what is now known as Project (Operation) STARGATE. He is well versed with developmental theory, methods of application, and current training technologies for remote viewing, as currently applied under strict laboratory controls and oversight.

During his career, Mr. McMoneagle has provided professional intelligence and creative/innovative informational support to the Central Intelligence Agency, Defense Intelligence Agency, National Security Agency, Drug Enforcement Agency, Secret Service, Federal Bureau of Investigation, United States Customs, the National Security Council, most major commands within the Department of Defense, and hundreds of other individuals, companies, and corporations. He is the only one who has successfully demonstrated his ability more than two dozen times, by doing a live remote viewing, double-blind and under controls while on-camera for national networks/labs in four countries.

Mr. McMoneagle has also been responsible for his Military Occupational Specialty at Army Headquarters level, to include control and management of both manned and unmanned sites within the Continental United States, and overseas. He was responsible for all tactical and strategic equipment tasking, including aircraft and vehicles, development of new and current technology, planning, support and maintenance, funding, training, and personnel. He has performed responsibly in international and intra-service negotiations and agreements in support of six national level intelligence agencies, and has acted as a direct consultant to the Commanding General, United States Army Intelligence and Security Command (INSCOM), Washington D.C., as well as the Army Chief of Staff for Intelligence (ACSI), Pentagon.

Other employment has included, Assistant to the Security Officer for a multi-billion dollar overseas intelligence facility, with responsibilities that included physical plant communications, personnel, and technology security; as well as counter-terrorist and counter-intelligence operations. He has served as the Detachment Commander at two remote intelligence collection sites overseas, providing field intelligence collection, analysis and reporting at theater, region, country, and city levels. He has also served on an Air and Sea Rescue team, in Long Range Reconnaissance, as a Quick Reaction Strike Force team leader, and rifleman. He has earned 28 military decorations and numerous awards…

"The 'giggle factor' associated with remote viewing or psychic functioning continues to block earnest attempts at using these functions for humankind's benefit."

Joseph McMoneagle ~ *The Ultimate Time Machine*

Human Use

Remote Viewing research may involve input from different sources as in the application of the Army's Human Use Policies developed to protect soldiers from abusive practices after accidental deaths occurred while serving.

"In February 1979, the General Counsel, the Army's top lawyer, declared [the RV Program named] Grill Flame activities constitute Human Use." The Unit, "... was in the middle of the [authorization] process in March 1979 when the Human Use determination was reversed by the Army Surgeon General's Human Use Subjects Research Review Board. Their decision...trumped the Army General Counsel's ruling..."

"On November 20, the Surgeon General's board changed its mind and decided that Grill Flame did indeed involve Human Use. It took until February 1, 1982 to get final approval from the Secretary of the Army (on the Joint Chiefs of Staff) to continue operations."[23]

New candidates were then issued a warning by a Major General before being accepted into the black-ops 902nd Intelligence Unit.

"Among other things, they noted that if the candidate joined the project, he would be exposed to psychic phenomena at a level and with a frequency that most people had never experienced before. As a result, he might change in certain ways. Ultimately, no harm should come to him, but he might have a new perspective on himself, his marriage, the universe. In a sense, he might become a new man, and a new husband."

The candidate and his wife were advised to talk, "...this over before they made the final commitment to go to Fort Meade."[24]

---

[23] Smith, Paul H., *Reading the Enemy's Mind – Inside Star Gate, America's Psychic Espionage Program*; Tor Non-fiction, 2005; p. 118

[24] Schnabel, Jim, *Remote Viewers*: *The Secret History of America's Psychic Spies*; Dell Non-Fiction, 1997, p. 270

A Chinese Encounter

The United States is not the only nation to study and use Remote Viewing. Below is a story allowing enthusiasts and skeptics alike a rare look at life inside the Unit during the middle 1980's.

The first time it happened was right after [Major] General Stubblebine had briefed me on the project and said that I would be contacted. The next week I was working mid shift, and one of the afternoons, I lay down for a nap. In that nap, I had a really shallow and lame dream about something I can't remember now. But at one point, right over the top of that dream there was what appeared to be a semi-translucent visual of three people.

One was a very respectable, businesslike slender man in a suit. A second was a very burly, stocky man, also in a suit, and with a very "Texas farmer" face. The third was an...Oriental girl... (I find it impossible to tell the age of oriental women). She was following along behind the two men and watching.

The men came up to me and talked about something, but I couldn't hear them. The girl was standing behind the two men, listening. The faces were very clear. Clear enough that when the two men actually came to [the INSCOM [Intelligence and Security Command] Base in Augsburg [Germany] to interview me, I recognized them immediately. I could have picked them out of a crowd on the sidewalk. I didn't think anything of the fact that the girl wasn't with them. It would have been odd to have her on a military trip overseas. I thought she was probably some-one in the unit.

Months later, when I got to the unit, she wasn't there. I asked about her and neither the director nor Joe [McMoneagle] (the two men who came to interview me) knew who I was talking about. I figured that it was just an AOL (a STRAY CAT) [the Sub-conscious Transfer of Recollections, Anxieties, and Yearnings to Consciously Accessible Thought] and blew it off.

About a year later, I was doing a practice target. The target was a museum at Arizona State University (I didn't know that only had numbers). I was describing things lying in glass topped cases, with the cases up on legs and stands, all arranged around the room for easy access, when I noticed that someone at the target site was looking straight at me, as though she could see me. It startled me, and for probably the only time ever, I wasn't startled OUT of the session, but deeper into it. I looked back at her, and realized that it was the same girl who had been following the director and Joe in my earlier "dream", back in Augsburg. I looked directly at her, and started to say hello, but then she realized that I could see her, too, and she half turned, and disappeared. That threw me out of the session.

Fortunately, [Captain] Paul Smith was my monitor, and ever the curious one, when I told him what had happened, he said, "Let's follow her and see where she went." Through a series of very impromptu movement commands, we finally located her back at the place where she worked ... the Chinese psychic intelligence effort.

She appeared in some of my sessions after that, but rarely. I tried to find her several times, and a few of them succeeded. Apparently, what they defined as "session" and what we defined as "session" weren't the same. Anyway, over time, we struck up somewhat of a stand-offish acquaintance. About a year after that, I hadn't bumped into her again, so I did a session specifically to find her. She was then in college in a very large city, and evidently out of the government's project altogether. When I found her, she acknowledged my presence, and very strongly desired that we not have further contact. I backed out of the session, and haven't tried again, since. Don't cha love war stories?"

Oct. 1, 1998 e-mail from Leonard Buchanan – Former Operational Database Manager 902nd Military Intelligence Unit - Fort Meade, Maryland and Owner of Problems>Solutions>Innovations, Inc.

----

[3] For more information, see, *China's Super Psychics* by Paul Dong and Thomas Raffill; Marlowe & Co. New York, 1997

Military Protocols

Surrounding the military's RV session protocols are the Operational Flow Protocols. The tasking agency was the "Customer" whose identity was strictly withheld to avoid inferences leading to Analytic Overlay. First published here, this process was highly classified for over two decades.

* * *

"In actual fact, there was pretty much a different work set-up every time we changed directors in the military unit which was pretty often as projects go. As a result, the "ideal plan" was never adhered to. Many times, we had to sort of switch horse in mid-stream. Anyway, here is the "ideal" workflow:

The **CUSTOMER** (Governmental Agency) comes to the unit director with a tasking.

The **UNIT DIRECTOR** meets with the customer and:

1) makes absolutely certain that the customer knows what CRV is and isn't – what it will and won't do.

2) looks the customer's problem over to see that it is the type of work we are best suited for. If not, he suggests a different solution for them.

If so, he then:

3) gets rid of the customer's "test" questions which only take up time and effort and accomplish nothing.

4) gets rid of the unnecessary questions – just fluff questions which the customer would like to have answered.

5) makes certain the questions asked are questions the customer really wants the answers to. There are LOTS of times when the customer will ask, "Who killed the victim", when the information he really wants is, "Where can we find the evidence that will show who killed the victim?"

6) agrees in writing on a set of basic questions which will be answered, once all the fluff and confusion is gotten out of the way.

7) makes certain that the Customer knows that these questions will be answered, and that other information will be provided, if it is found. However, if it isn't found, then the viewers are only responsible for what is being tasked. Follow-on questions will have to be asked later.

8) explains to the Customer the need for accurate feedback.
9) gets a definite commitment from the Customer that such feedback will be given, on each and every viewer's answer(s) to each and every question.
10) sets a commitment date for providing the answers. This must be a realistic date. Every Customer wants answers right now or yesterday, but the unit director needs to impress on the Customer that there are other customers who also have time limits of now or yesterday, and that reality must figure into the planning, like it or not.
11) provides the final list of questions to the Project Officer, along with any background information about the case gained from the customer.

The **PROJECT OFFICER** studies the background information and tasked questions and:
1) determines the main subject matter for each question.
2) decides the project number and fills out all the preliminary paperwork required for starting a new project.
3) provides the list of subjects to the Data Base Manager. The Data Base Manager looks up each information category in the data base and provides the Project Manager with a separate list of Viewers' names as suggested Viewers for each question.
4) determines which Viewers and Monitors should work on each question.
5) looks at the Viewers' and Monitors' existing schedules and determines the project's time line. He may even do a Pert chart to make scheduling easier.
6) “translates” each question into neutral wording.
7) notifies each Monitor and Viewer of the work schedule change.
8) generates an official tasking sheet to hand to each Monitor.

The **MONITOR** receives the tasking and coordinates from the Project Officer, along with any background information the Project Officer thinks the Monitor should know to help the Viewer better perform a productive session. The Monitor then:
1) makes certain he knows the Viewer's likes and dislikes, quirks, micro-movements, etc. If not, these are either looked up or found out from another Monitor who is more familiar with the Viewer.
2) gets information from the Database Manager about the Viewer's strengths and weaknesses. While this carries the danger of a “self-fulfilling prophecy”, the Monitor is hopefully trained enough to use

the information for formatting the session, rather than for guiding and leading the Viewer. If the Monitor is not this well trained, this step is passed up.
3) prepares the session workplace.
4) goes through the session with the Viewer.
5) helps the Viewer write the summary, if necessary.
6) after the paperwork is all done, provides both the Viewer's transcript and his (the Monitor's) session notes to the Analyst.

The **ANALYST** receives the paperwork and:
1) familiarizes himself with all the background knowledge.
2) collects the papers from all Viewer/Monitor pairs.
3) looks into his own notes on each and every Viewer to see work profiles (prone to using imagery, prone to using allegories, etc.). The Database Manager can be of help in this step.
4) performs analysis on the session (see the Analyst's Manual).
5) writes up his reports, critiques, summaries, etc. and provides it to the Report Writer.

The **REPORT WRITER** receives all the information from the Analyst and:
1) familiarizes himself with all the available background information.
2) familiarizes himself with all the Analyst's finding, interpretations and comments.
3) writes the final report (see the Report Writer's Manual)
NOTE!!! This includes taking the finalized answer to each Viewer to make certain that what is being reported is what the Viewer actually meant to say.
4) provides the final report to the Project Officer.

The **PROJECT OFFICER** then:
1) receives the finalized answers to each question after the session has been performed, analyzed and prepared for reporting.
2) gives final approval on the final report.
3) passes the final report to the Unit Director for delivery to the Customer.

The **UNIT DIRECTOR** then:
1) contacts the Customer and sets a date and time to go over the report. Information is not given ad hoc over the phone, nor is an "executive summary" provided.
2) meets with the Customer to provide the report.
3) once again makes certain that the Customer understands the

CRV process, strengths and limitations.
4) explains what happened, and how each answer was obtained.
5) points out to the Customer that each question has a "dependability rating" beside it which will tell the Customer what each Viewer's track record is on each specific answer to each type of question. He explains how this "dependability rating" can be used by the Customer as an aid to making decisions from the information provided.
6) sets – in writing – a hard and definite "drop dead" date for feedback.
7) if/when feedback comes in, provides it to the Project Officer who handled the case.
8) if feedback doesn't come in, or is received incorrectly, it is returned to the Customer to either, "dun him" for feedback, or to re-explain how feed-back needs to be provided, formatted, etc.

The **PROJECT OFFICER** then:
1) evaluates each Viewer's response to each question against the feedback.
2) provides an evaluation to each Viewer.
3) provides accurate data to the Database Manager for input into the database.
4) completes all summary paperwork for the project.
5) organizes all related paperwork, checks it for completeness, and prepares it for final storage and filing.

The **DATABASE MANAGER**:
1) inputs all received information into the database.
2) "massages" the database to provide information to those who need it. This includes the Training Officer and all Trainers.
3) maintains quality control on the data going in. "Garbage in – garbage out".

The **TRAINING OFFICER**:
1) schedules training times and facilities.
2) keeps evaluation reports on the Trainers.

The **TRAINER**:
1) accompanies new Viewers through the training process, analyzing their needs and progress every step of the way (see Trainers Manual).
2) makes and keeps records of the Viewer Student's "natural micro-movements". These will be provided to the Monitors along with a Viewer Student's profile of strengths and weakness.

3) advises management of the Viewer Student's progress and advises as to the student's best possible "training track" for providing the most useful and productive Viewer possible.

Needless to say, this is an overview, and not a complete list of responsibilities and obligations. For example, it doesn't cover what goes on in follow-on tasking, etc.

July 23, 1998 e-mail from: Leonard Buchanan– Former Operational Database Manager at the 902nd Military Intelligence Unit - Fort Meade, Maryland and Owner of Problems> Solutions>Innovations, Inc.

Interview Clarification

Question: Generally speaking, how much...information should be given a viewer in operations / applications?

Joseph McMoneagle: None. Zero. What you can do if the target requires a response or a description of an individual, you can say, "*Describe the individual at* (whatever location)" and the location needs to be hidden (would be a number, for instance). If you were targeting let's say a church, and there was an individual in that church, the church would be coded as say, "location A1". It would then say, "*describe individual at location A1*"'.

Under no condition can you give any information that is directly pertinent to the target. There is never any front-loading. The reason for this is because the entire concept of remote viewing is that an individual is forced, has no choice, but to use their psi ability to answer the requirement. Any info that is given in any way, or form, modifies that response in a way that removes / reduces the probability of accuracy.

Beginnings

This details the basis for the original black ops program funding. For readers interested in the data that justified Congressional spending for all those years, this overview of U.S. Military History is recommended.

CIA-Initiated Remote Viewing At Stanford Research Institute

by H. E. Puthoff, Ph.D.25
Institute for Advanced Studies at Austin
4030 Braker Lane W., #300
Austin, Texas 78759-5329

Abstract - In July 1995 the CIA declassified, and approved for release, documents revealing its sponsorship in the 1970s of a program at Stanford Research Institute in Menlo Park, CA, to determine whether such phenomena as remote viewing "might have any utility for intelligence collection" [1]. Thus began disclosure to the public of a two-decade-plus involvement of the intelligence community in the investigation of so-called para-psychological or psi phenomena. Presented here by the program's Founder and first Director (1972 - 1985) is the early history of the program, including discussion of some of the first, now declassified, results that drove early interest.

Introduction

On April 17, 1995, President Clinton issued Executive Order Nr. 1995-4-17, entitled Classified National Security Information. Although in one sense the order simply reaffirmed much of what has been long-standing policy, in another sense there was a clear

---

[25] Harold Puthoff received his BS and MS Degrees in Electrical Engineering at the University of Florida and a PhD from Stanford University in 1967. He went on to work at the National Security Agency at Fort Meade, Maryland as an Army engineer studying, lasers, high-speed computers, and fiber optics. He is the inventor of the tunable infra-red laser. He spent three years as a naval officer and worked eight years in the Microwave Laboratory at Stanford. Puthoff has over 31 technical papers published on such topics as electron-beam devices, lasers and quantum zero-point-energy effects. He reportedly has patents issued in the areas of energy fields, laser, and communications. [author]

shift toward more openness. In the opening paragraph, for example, we read: "In recent years, however, dramatic changes have altered, although not eliminated, the national security threats that we confront. These changes provide a greater opportunity to emphasize our commitment to open Government." In the Classification Standards section of the Order this commitment is operationalized by phrases such as "If there is significant doubt about the need to classify information, it shall not be classified." Later in the document, in reference to information that requires continued protection, there even appears the remarkable phrase "In some exceptional cases, however, the need to protect such information may be outweighed by the public interest in disclosure of the information, and in these cases the information should be declassified."

A major fallout of this reframing of attitude toward classification is that there is enormous pressure on those charged with maintaining security to work hard at being responsive to reasonable requests for disclosure. One of the results is that FOIA (Freedom of Information Act) requests that have languished for months to years are suddenly being acted upon.[1]

One outcome of this change in policy is the government's recent admission of its two-decade-plus involvement in funding highly-classified, special access programs in remote viewing (RV) and related psi phenomena, first at Stanford Research Institute (SRI) and then at Science Applications International Corporation (SAIC), both in Menlo Park, CA, supplemented by various in-house government programs. Although almost all of the documentation remains yet classified, in July 1995 270 pages of SRI reports were declassified and released by the CIA, the program's first sponsor [2]. Thus, although through the years columns by Jack Anderson and others had claimed leaks of "psychic spy" programs with such exotic names as Grill Flame, Center Lane, Sunstreak and Star Gate, CIA's release of the SRI reports constitutes the first documented public admission of significant intelligence community involvement in the psi area.

As a consequence of the above, although I had founded the program in early 1972, and had acted as its Director until I left in 1985 to head up the Institute for Advanced Studies at Austin (at which point my colleague Ed May assumed responsibility as Director), it was not until 1995 that I found myself for the first time able to utter in a single sentence the connected acronyms CIA/SRI/RV. In this report I discuss the genesis of the program, report on some of the early, now declassified, results that drove early interest, and outline the general direction the program took as it expanded into a multi-year, multi-site, multi-million-dollar effort to determine whether such phenomena as remote viewing "might have any utility for intelligence collection" [1].

Beginnings

In early 1972, I was involved in laser research at Stanford Research Institute (now called SRI International) in Menlo Park, CA. At that time I was also circulating a proposal to obtain a small grant for some research in quantum biology. In that proposal I had raised the issue whether physical theory as we knew it was capable of describing life processes, and had suggested some measurements involving plants and lower organisms [3]. This proposal was widely circulated, and a copy was sent to Cleve Backster in New York City who was involved in measuring the electrical activity of plants with standard polygraph equipment. New York artist Ingo Swann chanced to see my proposal during a visit to Backster's lab, and wrote me suggesting that if I were interested in investigating the boundary between the physics of the animate and inanimate, I should consider experiments of the parapsychological type. Swann then went on to describe some apparently successful experiments in psychokinesis in which he had participated at Prof. Gertrude Schmeidler's laboratory at the City College of New York. As a result of this correspondence I invited him to visit SRI for a week in June 1972 to demonstrate such effects, frankly, as much out of personal scientific curiosity as anything else.

Prior to Swann's visit I arranged for access to a well-shielded magneto-meter used in a quark-detection experiment in the Physics Department at Stanford University. During our visit to this laboratory, sprung as a surprise to Swann, he appeared to perturb the operation of the magnetometer, located in a vault below the floor of the building and shielded by mu-metal shielding, an aluminum container, copper shielding and a superconducting shield. As if to add insult to injury, he then went on to "remote view" the interior of the apparatus, rendering by drawing a reasonable facsimile of its rather complex (and heretofore unpublished) construction. It was this latter feat that impressed me perhaps even more than the former, as it also eventually did representatives of the intelligence community. I wrote up these observations and circulated it among my scientific colleagues in draft form of what was eventually published as part of a conference proceeding [4].

In a few short weeks a pair of visitors showed up at SRI with the above report in hand. Their credentials showed them to be from the CIA. They knew of my previous background as a Naval Intelligence Officer and then civilian employee at the National Security Agency (NSA) several years earlier, and felt they could discuss their concerns with me openly. There was, they told me, increasing concern in the intelligence community about the level of effort in Soviet parapsychology being funded by the Soviet security services [5]; by Western scientific standards the field was considered nonsense by most working scientists. As a result they had been on the lookout for a research laboratory outside of academia that could handle a quiet, low-profile classified investigation, and SRI appeared to fit the bill. They asked if I could arrange an opportunity for them to carry out some simple experiments with Swann, and, if the tests proved satisfactory, would I consider a pilot program along these lines? I agreed to consider this, and arranged for the requested tests. [2]

The tests were simple, the visitors simply hiding objects in a box and asking Swann to attempt to describe the contents. The results generated in these experiments are perhaps captured most eloquently by the following example. In one test Swann said "I see something small, brown and irregular, sort of like a leaf or something that resembles it, except that it seems very much alive, like it's even moving!" The target chosen by one of the visitors turned out to be a small live moth, which indeed did look like a leaf. Although not all responses were quite so precise, nonetheless the integrated results were sufficiently impressive that in short order an eight-month, $49,909 Biofield Measurements Program was negotiateed as a pilot study, a laser colleague Russell Targ who had had a long-time interest and involvement in parapsychology joined the program, and the experimental effort was begun in earnest.

Early Remote Viewing Results

During the eight-month pilot study of remote viewing the

effort gradually evolved from the remote viewing of symbols and objects in envelopes and boxes, to the remote viewing of local target sites in the San Francisco Bay area, demarked by outbound experimenters sent to the site under strict protocols devised to prevent artifactual results. Later judging of the results were similarly handled by double-blind protocols designed to foil artifactual matching. Since these results have been presented in detail elsewhere, both in the scientific literature [6-8] and in popular book format [9], I direct the interested reader to these sources. To summarize, over the years the back-and-forth criticism of protocols, refinement of methods, and successful replication of this type of remote viewing in independent laboratories [10-14], has yielded considerable scientific evidence for the reality of the phenomenon. Adding to the strength of these results was the discovery that a growing number of individuals could be found to demonstrate high-quality remote viewing, often to their own surprise, such as the talented Hella Hammid. As a separate issue, however, most convincing to our early program monitors were the results now to be described, generated under their own control.

First, during the collection of data for a formal remote viewing series targeting indoor laboratory apparatus and outdoor locations (a series eventually published in toto in the Proc. IEEE [7]), the CIA contract monitors, ever watchful for possible chicanery, participated as remote viewers themselves in order to critique the protocols. In this role three separate viewers, designated visitors V1 - V3 in the IEEE paper, contributed seven of the 55 viewings, several of striking quality. Reference to the IEEE paper for a comparison of descriptions/ drawings to pictures of the associated targets, generated by the contract monitors in their own viewings, leaves little doubt as to why the contract monitors came to the conclusion that there was something to remote viewing (see, for example, Figure 1 herein).

As summarized in the Executive Summary of the now-released Final Report [2] of the second year of the program, "The development of this capability at SRI has evolved to the point where visiting CIA personnel with no previous exposure to such concepts have performed well under controlled laboratory conditions (that is, generated target descriptions of sufficiently high quality to permit blind matching of descriptions to targets by independent judges)." What happened next, however, made even these results pale in comparison.

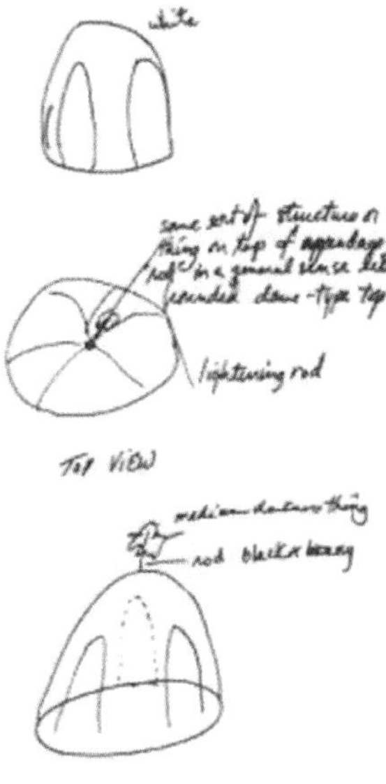

Figure 1 – Sketch of target by VI

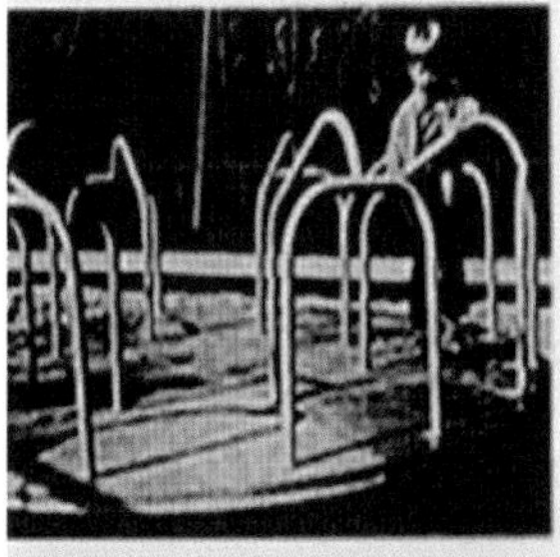

Figure 2 – Target (merry-go-round)

Coordinate Remote Viewing

To determine whether it was necessary to have a "beacon" individual at the target site, Swann suggested carrying out an experiment to remote view the planet Jupiter before the upcoming NASA Pioneer 10 fly by. In that case, much to his chagrin (and ours) he found a ring around Jupiter, and wondered if perhaps he had remote viewed Saturn by mistake. Our colleagues in astronomy were quite unimpressed as well, until the flyby revealed that an unanticipated ring did in fact exist. [3] Expanding the protocols yet further, Swann proposed a series of experiments in which the target was designated not by sending a "beacon" person to the target site, but rather by the use of geographical coordinates, latitude and longitude in degrees, minutes and seconds. Needless to say, this proposal seemed even more outrageous than "ordinary" remote viewing. The difficulties in taking this proposal seriously, designing protocols to eliminate the possibility of a combination of globe memorization and eidetic or photographic memory, and so forth, are discussed in considerable detail in Reference [9]. Suffice it to say that investigation of this approach, which we designated Scanate (scanning by coordinate), eventually provided us with sufficient evidence to bring it up to the contract monitors and suggest a test under their control. A description of that test and its results, carried out in mid-1973 during the initial pilot study, are best presented by quoting directly from the Executive Summary of the Final Report of the second year's follow-up program [2]. The remote viewers were Ingo Swann and Pat Price, and the entire transcripts are available in the released documents [2].

In order to subject the remote viewing phenomena to a rigorous long distance test under external control, a request for geographical coordinates of a site unknown to subject and experimenters was forwarded to the OSI group responsible for threat analysis in this area. In response, SRI personnel received a set of geographical coordinates (latitude and longitude in degrees, minutes, and seconds) of a facility, hereafter referred to as the West Virginia Site. The experimenters then carried out a remote viewing experiment on a double-blind basis, that is, blind to experimenters as well as subject. The experiment had as its goal the determination of the utility of remote viewing under conditions approximating an operational scenario. Two subjects targeted on the site, a sensitive installation. One subject drew a detailed map of the building and grounds layout, the other provided information about the interior including code words, data subsequently verified by sponsor sources (report available from COTR).[4]

Since details concerning the site's mission in general, [5] and evaluation of the remote viewing test in particular, remain highly classified to this day, all that can be said is that interest in the client community was heightened considerably following this exercise.

Because Price found the above exercise so interesting, as a personal challenge he went on to scan the other side of the globe for a Communist Bloc equivalent and found one located in the Urals, the detailed description of which is also included in Ref. [2]. As with the West Virginia Site, the report for the Urals Site was also verified by personnel in the sponsor organization as being substantially correct.

What makes the West Virginia/Urals Sites viewings so remarkable is that these are not best-ever examples culled out of a longer list; these are literally the first two site-viewings carried out in a simulated operational-type scenario. In fact, for Price these were the very first two remote viewings in our program altogether, and he was invited to participate in yet further experimentation.

Operational Remote Viewing (Semipalatinsk, USSR)

Midway through the second year of the program (July 1974) our CIA sponsor decided to challenge us to provide data on a Soviet site of ongoing operational significance. Pat Price was the remote viewer. A description of the remote viewing, taken from our declassified final report [2], reads as given below. I cite this level of detail to indicate the thought that goes into such an "experiment" to minimize cueing while at the same time being responsive to the requirements of an operational situation. Again, this is not a "best-ever" example from a series of such viewings, but rather the very first operational Soviet target concerning which we were officially tasked. "To determine the utility of remote viewing under operational conditions, a long-distance remote viewing experiment was carried out on a sponsor designated target of current interest, an unidentified research center at Semipalatinsk, USSR.

This experiment, carried out in three phases, was under direct control of the COTR. To begin the experiment, the COTR furnished map coordinates in degrees, minutes and seconds. The only additional information provided was the designation of the target as an R&D test facility. The experimenters then closeted themselves with Subject S1, gave him the map coordinates and indicated the designation of the target as an R&D test facility. A remote-viewing experiment was then carried out. This activity constituted Phase I of the experiment.

Figure 3 shows the subject's graphic effort for building layout; Figure 4 shows the subject's particular attention to a multistory gantry crane he observed at the site. Both results were obtained by the experimenters on a double-blind basis before exposure to any additional COTR-held information, thus eliminating the possibility of cueing. These results were turned over to the client representatives for evaluation. For comparison, an artist's rendering of the site as known to the COTR (but not to the experimenters until later) is shown in Figure 5.

Were the results not promising, the experiment would have stopped at this point. Description of the multistory crane, however, a relatively unusual target item, was taken as indicative of possible target acquisition. Therefore, Phase II was begun, defined by the subject being made "witting" (of the client) by client representatives who introduced themselves to the subject at that point; Phase II also included a second round of experimentation on the Semipalatinsk site with direct participation of client representtatives in which further data were obtained and evaluated. As preparation for this phase, client representatives purposely kept themselves blind to all but general knowledge of the target site to minimize the possibility of cueing. The Phase II effort was focused on the generation of physical data that could be independently verified by other client sources, thus providing a calibration of the process.

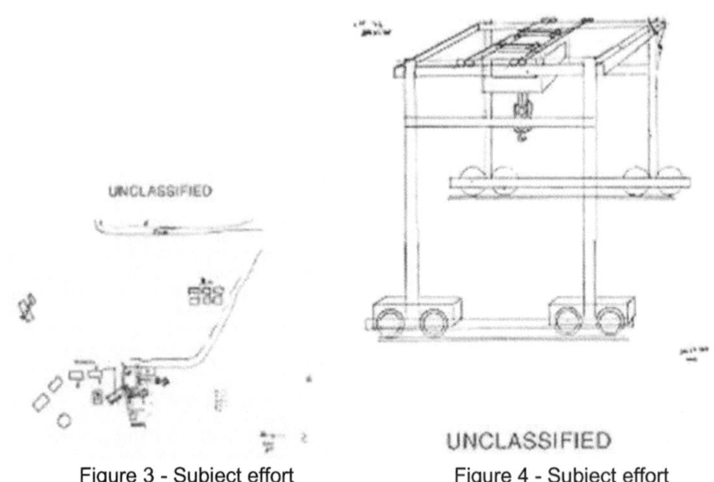

Figure 3 - Subject effort at building layout

Figure 4 - Subject effort construction crane

The end of Phase II gradually evolved into the first part of Phase III, the generation of unverifiable data concerning the Semipalatinsk site not available to the client, but of operational interest nonetheless. Several hours of tape transcript and a notebook of drawings were generated over a two-week period.

The data describing the Semipalatinsk site were evaluated by the sponsor, and are contained in a separate report. In general, several details concerning the salient technology of the Semipalatinsk site appeared to dovetail with data from other sources, and a number of specific large structural elements were correctly described. The results contained noise along with the signal, but were nonetheless clearly differentiated from the chance results that were generated by control subjects in comparison experiments carried out by the COTR."

For discussion of the ambiance and personal factors involved in carrying out this experiment, along with further detail generated as Price (see Figure 6) "roamed" the facility, including detailed comparison of Price's RV-generated information with later determined "ground-truth reality," see the accompanying article by Russell Targ in the Journal of Scientific Exploration <http:// www. jse.com/>, Vol. 10, No. 1.

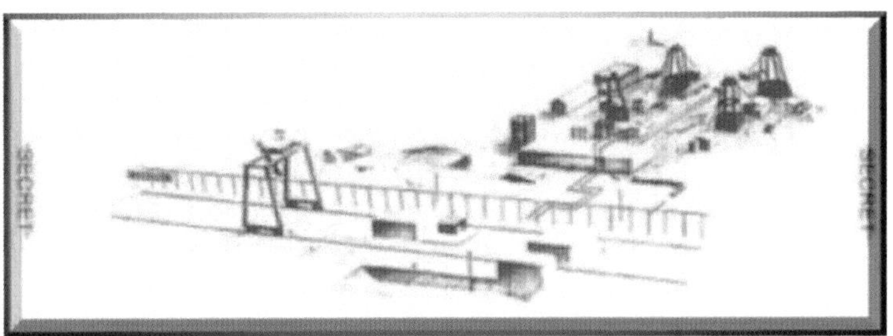

Figure 5 - Actual COTR rendering of Semipalatinsk, USSR target site.

Additional experiments having implications for intelligence concerns were carried out, such as the remote viewing of cipher machine type apparatus, and the RV-sorting of sealed envelopes to differentiate those that contained letters with secret writing from those that did not. To discuss these here in detail would take us too far afield, but the interested reader can follow up by referring to the now-declassified project documents [2].

Follow-on Programs

The above discussion brings us up to the end of 1975. As a result of the material being generated by both SRI and CIA remote viewers, interest in the program in government circles, especially within the intelligence community, intensified considerably and led to an ever increasing briefing schedule. This in turn led to an ever-increasing number of clients, contracts and tasking, and therefore expansion of the program to a multi-client base, and eventually to an integrated joint-services program under single-agency (DIA)[6] leadership. To meet the demand for the increased level of effort we first increased our professional staff by inviting Ed May to join the program in 1976, then screened and added to the program a cadre of remote viewers as consultants, and let subcontracts to increase our scope of activity.

Figure 6 - Left to right: Christopher Green, [26] Pat Price,[27] and Hal Puthoff . Picture taken following a successful experiment involving glider-ground RV.

As the program expanded, in only a very few cases could the client's identities and program tasking be revealed. Examples include a NASA-funded study negotiated early in the program by Russ Targ to determine whether the internal state of an electronic random-number-generator could be detected by RV processes [16], and a study funded by the Naval Electronics Systems Command to determine whether attempted remote viewing of distant light flashes would induce correlated changes in the viewer's brainwave (EEG) production [17]. For essentially all other projects, during my 14-yr. tenure at SRI, however, the identity of the clients and most of the tasking were classified and remain so today. (The exception was the occasional privately funded study.) We are told,

[26] Dr. Christopher Green MD. Neurophysiology, received the CIA's National Intelligence Medal as a Scientific Advisory Board Member to the CIA's Directorate of Intelligence.

[27] One of the finest remote viewers ever, Pat Price, a former police commissioner and councilman in Burbank, CA, came to the Government's attention when he viewed officers, interiors, and files at the virtually unknown, nuclear hardened Naval Satellite Intelligence site in West Virginia. When the Pentagon was shown the data, Price was interrogated by the U.S. Defense Investigative Service who demanded to know who had breached security and how they did it. He is reputed to be the only viewer that could read numbers and letters on a target. Later he viewed inside the Soviet installation at Mount Narodnaya in the Ural Mountains. He went on to work for the CIA and is reputed to have died of a heart attack in July of 1975, in Las Vegas. Even though he was supposedly dead on arrival at the hospital, no autopsy was performed. Suspicions have always existed about the truth of his death. [author]

however, that further declassification and release of much of this material is almost certain to occur.

What can be said, then, about further development of the program in the two decades following 1975?[7] In broad terms it can be said that much of the SRI effort was directed not so much toward developing an operational U.S. capability, but rather toward assessing the threat potential of its use against the U.S. by others.

The words 'threat assessment' were often used to describe the program's purpose during its development, especially during the early years. As a result, much of the remote-viewing activity was carried out under conditions where ground-truth reality was a priori known or could be determined, such as the description of U.S. facilities and technological developments, the timing of rocket test firings and underground nuclear tests, and the location of individuals and mobile units. And, of course, we were responsive to requests to provide assistance during such events as the loss of an airplane or the taking of hostages, relying on the talents of an increasing cadre of remote-viewer/ consultants, some well-known in the field such as Keith Harary, and many who have not surfaced publicly until recently, such as Joe McMoneagle.

One might ask whether in this program RV-generated information was ever of sufficient significance as to influence decisions at a policy level. This is of course impossible to determine unless policymakers were to come forward with a statement in the affirmative. One example of a possible candidate is a study we performed at SRI during the Carter administration debates concerning proposed deployment of the mobile MX missile system. In that scenario missiles were to be randomly shuffled from silo to silo in a silo field, in a form of high-tech shell game. In a computer simulation of a twenty-silo field with randomly-assigned (hidden) missile locations, we were able, using RV-generated data, to show rather forcefully that the application of a sophisticated statistical averaging technique (sequential sampling) could in principle permit an adversary to defeat the system. I briefed these results to the appropriate offices at their request, and a written report with the technical details was widely circulated among groups responsible for threat analysis [18], and with some impact. What role, if any, our small contribution played in the mix of factors behind the enormously complex decision to cancel the program will probably never be known, and must of course a priori be considered in all likelihood negligible. Nonetheless, this is a prototypical example of the kind of tasking that by its nature potentially had policy implications.

Even though the details of the broad range of experiments, some brilliant successes, many total failures, have not yet been released, we have nonetheless been able to publish summaries of what was learned in these studies about the overall characteristics of remote viewing, as in Table 5 of Reference [8]. Furthermore, over the years we were able to address certain questions of scientific interest in a rigorous way and to publish the results in the open literature. Examples include the apparent lack of attenuation of remote viewing due to seawater shielding (submersible experiments) [8], the amplification of RV performance by use of error-correcting coding techniques [19, 20], and the utility of a technique we call associational remote viewing (ARV) to generate useful predictive information [21].8

As a sociological aside, we note that the overall efficacy of remote viewing in a program like this was not just a scientific issue. For example, when the Semipalatinsk data described earlier was forwarded for analysis, one group declined to get involved because the whole concept was unscientific nonsense, while a second group declined because, even though it might be real, it was possibly demonic; a third group had to be found. And, as in the case of public debate about such phenomena, the program's image was on occasion as likely to be damaged by an over enthusiastic supporter, as by a detractor. Personalities, politics and personal biases were always factors to be dealt with.

Official Statements/Perspectives

With regard to admission by the government of its use of remote viewers under operational conditions, officials have on occasion been relatively forthcoming. President Carter, in a speech to college students in Atlanta in September 1995, is quoted by Reuters as saying that during his administration a plane went down in Zaire, and a meticulous sweep of the African terrain by American spy satellites failed to locate any sign of the wreckage. It was then "without my knowledge" that the head of the CIA (Adm. Stansfield Turner) turned to a woman reputed to have psychic powers. As told by Carter, "she gave some latitude and longitude figures. We focused our satellite cameras on that point and the plane was there." Independently, Turner himself also has admitted the Agency's use of a remote viewer (in this case, Pat Price).[9] And recently, in a segment taped for the British television series Equinox [22], Maj. Gen. Ed Thompson, Assistant Chief of Staff for Intelligence, U.S. Army (1977-1981), volunteered "I had one or more briefings by SRI and was impressed.... The decision I made was to set up a small, in-house, low-cost effort in remote viewing."

Finally, a recent unclassified report [23] prepared for the CIA by the American Institutes for Research (AIR), concerning a remote viewing effort carried out under a DIA program called Star Gate (discussed in detail elsewhere in this volume), cites the roles of the CIA and DIA in the history of the program, including acknowledgment that a cadre of full-time government employees used remote viewing techniques to respond to tasking from operational military organizations. [10]

As information concerning the various programs spawned by intelligence-community interest is released, and the dialog concerning their scientific and social significance is joined, the results are certain to be hotly debated. Bearing witness to this fact are the companion articles in this volume by Ed May, Director of the SRI and SAIC programs since 1985, and by Jessica Utts and Ray Hyman, consultants on the AIR evaluation cited above. These articles address in part the AIR study. That study, limited in scope to a small fragment of the overall program effort, resulted in a conclusion that although laboratory research showed statistically significant results, use of remote viewing in intelligence gathering was not warranted.

Regardless of one's a priori position, however, an unimpassioned observer cannot help but attest to the following fact. Despite the ambiguities inherent in the type of exploration covered in these programs, the integrated results appear to provide unequivocal evidence of a human capacity to access events remote in space and time, however falteringly, by some cognitive process not yet understood. My years of involvement as a research manager in these programs have left me with the conviction that this fact must be taken into account in any attempt to develop an unbiased picture of the structure of reality.

Footnotes

1 - One example being the release of documents that are the subject of this report - see the memoir by Russell Targ.

2 - Since the reputation of the intelligence services is mixed among members of the general populace, I have on occasion been challenged as to why I would agree to cooperate with the CIA or other elements of the intelligence community in this work. My answer is simply that as a result of my own previous exposure to this community I became persuaded that war can almost always be traced to a failure in intelligence, and that therefore the strongest weapon for peace is good intelligence.

3 - This result was published by us in advance of the ring's discovery [9].

4 - Editor's footnote added here: COTR - Contracting Officer's Technical Representative.

5 - An NSA listening post at the Navy's Sugar Grove facility, according to intelligence-community chronicler Bamford [15]

6 - DIA - Defense Intelligence Agency. The CIA dropped out as a major player in the mid-seventies due to pressure on the Agency (unrelated to the RV Program) from the Church-Pike Congressional Committee.

7 - See also the contribution by Ed May elsewhere in this volume concerning his experiences from 1985 on during his tenure as Director.

8 - For example, one application of this technique yielded not only a published, statistically significant result, but also a return of $26,000 in 30 days in the silver futures market [21].

9 - The direct quote is given in Targ's contribution elsewhere in this volume.

10 - "From 1986 to the first quarter of FY 1995, the DoD para-normal psychology program received more than 200 tasks from operational military organizations requesting that the program staff apply a paranormal psychological technique know (sic) as "remote viewing" (RV) to attain information unavailable from other sources." [23]

References

[1] "CIA Statement on 'Remote Viewing," CIA Public Affairs Office, 6 September 1995.

[2] Harold E. Puthoff and Russell Targ, "Perceptual Augmentation Techniques," SRI Progress Report No. 3 (31 Oct. 1974) and Final Report (1 Dec. 1975) to the CIA, covering the period January 1974 through February 1975, the second year of the program. This effort was funded at the level of $149,555.

[3] H. E. Puthoff, "Toward a Quantum Theory of Life Process," unpubl proposal, Stanford Research Institute (1972).

[4] H. E. Puthoff and R. Targ, "Physics, Entropy and Psycho-kinesis," in Proc. Conf. Quantum Physics and Parapsychology (Geneva, Switzerland); (New York: Parapsychology Foundation, 1975).

[5] Documented in "Paraphysics R&D - Warsaw Pact (U)," DST-1810S-202-78, Defense Intelligence Agency (30 March 1978).

[6] R. Targ and H. E. Puthoff, "Information Transfer under Conditions of Sensory Shielding," Nature 252, 602 (1974).

[7] H. E. Puthoff and R. Targ, "A Perceptual Channel for Information Transfer over Kilometer Distances: Historical Perspective and Recent Research," Proc. IEEE 64, 329 (1976).

[8] H. E. Puthoff, R. Targ and E. C. May, "Experimental Psi Research: Implications for Physics," in The Role of Consciousness in the Physical World", edited by R. G. Jahn (AAAS Selected Symposium 57, Westview Press, Boulder, 1981).
[9] R. Targ and H. E. Puthoff, Mind Reach (Delacorte Press, New York, 1977).
[10] J. P. Bisaha and B. J. Dunne, "Multiple Subject and Long-Distance Precognitive Remote Viewing of Geographical Locations," in Mind at Large, edited by C. T. Tart, H. E. Puthoff and R. Targ (Praeger, New York, 1979), p. 107.
[11] B. J. Dunne and J. P. Bisaha, "Precognitive Remote Viewing in the Chicago Area: a Replication of the Stanford Experiment," J. Parapsychology 43, 17 (1979).
[12] R. G. Jahn, "The Persistent Paradox of Psychic Phenomena: An Engineering Perspective," Proc. IEEE 70, 136 (1982).
[13] R. G. Jahn and B. J. Dunne, "On the Quantum Mechanics of Consciousness with Application to Anomalous Phenomena," Found. Phys. 16, 721 (1986).
[14] R. G. Jahn and B. J. Dunne, Margins of Reality (Harcourt, Brace and Jovanovich, New York, 1987).
[15] J. Bamford, The Puzzle Palace (Penguin Books, New York, 1983) pp. 218-222.
[16] R. Targ, P. Cole and H. E. Puthoff, "Techniques to Enhance Man/ Machine Communication," Stanford Research Institute Final Report on NASA Project NAS7-100 (August 1974).
[17] R. Targ, E. C. May, H. E. Puthoff, D. Galin and R. Ornstein, "Sensing of Remote EM Sources (Physiological Correlates)," SRI Intern'l Final Report on Naval Electronics Systems Command Project N00039-76-C-0077, covering the period November 1975 - to October 1976 (April 1978).
[18] H. E. Puthoff, "Feasibility Study on the Vulnerability of the MPS System to RV Detection Techniques," SRI Internal Report, 15 April 1979; revised 2 May 1979.
[19] H. E. Puthoff, "Calculator-Assisted Psi Amplification," Research in Parapsychology 1984, edited by Rhea White and J. Solfvin (Scarecrow Press, Metuchen, NJ, 1985), p. 48.
[20] H. E. Puthoff, "Calculator-Assisted Psi Amplification II: Use of the Sequential-Sampling Technique as a Variable-Length Majority-Vote Code," Research in Parapsychology 1985, edited by D. Weiner and D. Radin (Scarecrow Press, Metuchen, NJ, 1986), p. 73.
[21] H. E. Puthoff, "ARV (Associational Remote Viewing) Applications," Research in Parapsychology 1984, edited by Rhea White and J. Solfvin (Scarecrow Press, Metuchen, NJ, 1985), p. 121.
[22] "The Real X-Files", Independent Channel 4, England (shown 27 August 1995); to be shown in the U.S. on the Discovery Channel.
[23] M. D. Mumford, A. M. Rose and D. Goslin, "An Evaluation of Remote Viewing: Research and Applications", American Institutes for Research (September 29, 1995).

[The footnotes were designed to facilitate a greater understanding of Remote Viewing pioneers, but are not original. Dr. Puthoff's text was not altered.]

Targeted Reading

Because of its capabilities, Remote Viewing disinformation exists that discourages further interest. This list was compiled to help people search for media from members of the military program

McMoneagle, Joseph W.
- *Mind Trek*; Hampton Roads, 1993
- *The Ultimate Time Machine*; Hampton Roads, 1998
- *Remote Viewing Secrets*; Hampton Roads, 2000
- *The Stargate Chronicles*; Hampton Roads, 2002
- *Memoirs of a Psychic Spy: The Remarkable Life of U. S. Government Remote Viewer 001*; Hampton Roads, 2006

Buchanan, Leonard
- *The Seventh Sense – The Secrets of Remote Viewing as Told by a "Psychic Spy" for the U.S. Military*; Paraview Pocket Books, 2003
- *Remote Viewing Methods - Remote Viewing and Remote Influencing*; DVD, 2004

Smith, Paul H.
- *Reading the Enemy's Mind - Inside Stargate - America's Psychic Espionage Program*; Tor non-fiction, 2005

Morehouse, David A.
- *Psychic Warrior – Inside the CIA's Stargate Program: The True Story of a Soldiers Espionage and Awakening*; St Martin's Press, 1996
- *Nonlethal Weapons: War Without Death*; Praeger Publishers, 1996
- *Remote Viewing: The Complete User's Manual for Coordinate Remote Viewing*; Sounds True Publishers, 2011

Atwater, F. Holmes
- *Captain of My Ship, Master of My Soul: Living with Guidance*; Hampton Roads Publishing, 2001

Puthoff, Harold E. with Targ, Russell
- *Mind Reach - Scientists Look at Psychic Abilities*; Delacorte, 1977 & New World Library, 2004

Swann, Ingo
- *To Kiss the Earth Goodbye*; Hawthorne, New York, 1975
- *Star Fire*, Dell non-fiction, 1978

- *Everybody's Guide to Natural ESP: Unlocking the Extrasensory Power of Your Mind*; Jeremy P. Tharcher Imprint, 1991
- *Your Nostradamus Factor*; Fireside Press, 1993
- *Remote Viewing & ESP From The Inside Out*; DVD

Targ, Russell
- *Mind Race: Understanding and Using Psychic Abilities*, with Keith Harary; Ballantine Books, 1984
- *Miracles of Mind: Exploring Nonlocal Consciousness and Spiritual Healing*; New World Library, 1999
- *Limitless Mind: A Guide to Remote Viewing and Transformation of Consciousness*; New World Library, 2004

Other Sources
- Schnabel, Jim – *Remote Viewers: The Secret History of America's Psychic Spies*; Dell–non-fiction, 1997

- McRae, Ronald – *Mind Wars: The true story of Government Research into the Military Potential of Psychic Weapons*; St Martin's Press, 1984

- Radin, Dean - *Entangled Minds: Extrasensory Experiences in a Quantum Reality*, Paraview Pocket Books, 2006

- Gruber, Elmar – *Psychic Wars – Parapsychology in Espionage – and Beyond*; Blandford, London, 1999

- Dong, Paul with Thomas Rafill – *China's Super Psychics*; Marlowe & Co., New York, 1997

Additional Taskings

Lae City Airport, New Guinea - July 1937 – Get into the cockpit for the last flight of the vanished pilot Amelia Earhart. Learn of the plane's unknown final flight trajectory, cockpit circumstances and final thoughts in her last minute of life. Entered into four libraries within six months, including Purdue University's Earhart Special Collection Library, the book includes a "how to find the debris field" location map with yardages and points of reference including a flight scenario that has never been put forward. With the failure of the TIGHAR Group in 2012, insiders have subsequently blogged that the Southeast end scenario is the one worth investigating.

Onboard RMS Titanic - North Atlantic - April 1912 – In

the first book to appear since the 2nd Officer's granddaughter's revelations, review the Evidential Details substantiating the amazing crow's nest developments as Titanic bore down on the ice. Then, move to a resolution regarding Captain E. J. Smith's final actions in his previously unknown non-drowning death. The book includes obscure artifact drawings whose existence was only confirmed through ocean floor salvage after the remote viewing sessions. Read History's only narrative of the last unknown 20 minutes as the radical tilt prepared to take over 1500 terrified travelers down into the frigid ocean at 2:18 in the morning.

The Civil War, State of Maryland - September 1862 – Considered an unsolvable whodunit, this little known, but most significant mystery in America's Civil War resolves who lost Confederate General Robert E. Lee's top-secret Special Order 191. The result was the battles of South Mountain and Harper's Ferry, leading directly to the bloodiest day in American History at Antietam Creek. The upshot was the timing of the Emancipation Proclamation that legalized the election of Barak Obama. With information from the National Park Service, the book provides aerial campground maps and reveals the previously unknown who, why, when, where and how these orders found their way into the Union General's hands. This book also provides the world's first clinical determination on Union Commander George McClellan's psychological problems.

Last Stand Hill - Little Big Horn River - Montana - June, 1876 – This is History's only documentation of **General George Armstrong Custer**'s last stand from the viewpoints of the victors and the vanquished. Read about Chief Sitting Bull's as well as Custer's battle thoughts. Learn of his true cause of Custer's death and the amazing reasons his body is likely not in his tomb at West Point. You get new, remote viewing generated, battle maps with a drawing of Custer's last fighting stance, a near death facial close-up drawing and, since he was never photographed, the world's only full page color portrait of Indian War Chief *Crazy Horse*.

Princess Diana References

[i] McMoneagle, Joseph W., *Remote Viewing Secrets – A Handbook*; Hampton Roads Publishing Company, Inc. 2000 p. xv
[ii] McMoneagle, Joseph W., *The Stargate Chronicles*; Hampton Roads Publishing Company, Inc. 2002 p. 182
[iii] Simmons, Simone, *Diana – The Secret Years* with Susan Hill; Ballantine Books 1998 p.120
[iv] Delorm, Rene, *Diana & Dodi - A Love Story - By the Butler Who Saw Their Romance Blossom*, with Barry Fox and Nadine Taylor; Tallfellow Press 1998 p.144
[v] Anderson, Christopher, *The Day Diana Died;* William Morrow and Company 1998 p.114
[vi] Anderson; p.113
[vii] Delorm; p.154
[viii] ibid; p.154
[ix] The Learning Channel Presentation - *Princess Diana*; A Fulcrum Production; a Granada Presentation for ITV 1998; hereafter referred to as *TLC*
[x] Delorm; p.155
[xi] Anderson; p.99
[xii] ibid; p.166
[xiii] Sancton, Thomas and Scott MacLeod, *Death of a Princess - The Investigation*; St. Martin's Press 1998 p.157
[xiv] Delorm; p.157
[xv] ibid; p.158
[xvi] Spoto, Donald, *Diana - The Last Year*;; Harmony Books 1997 p. 171
[xvii] Sanction; p.158-9
[xviii] TLC - Mohammed Al-Fayed interview
[xix] Junor, Penny, *Charles - Victim or Villain*; Harper Collins Publishers 1998; p.18
[xx] Sanction; p.167
[xxi] Final Report - Paris Prosecutor's Office; Head of the Prosecution Department at Courts of the First Instance; Examining Magistrates Hervé Stephan and Christine Devidal
[xxii] *TLC* - documentary information
[xxiii] *TLC* - interview with Dr. Martin Skinner.
[xxiv] Anderson; p.191
[xxv] Interview with Mohammed Al Fayed as per his internet site address: www.alfayed.com/indexie4.html, as published to the Internet on October 25, 1998
[xxvi] Spoto; p.172
[xxvii] Sanction; p 251
[xxviii] ibid; p. 6
[xxix] *Newsweek* Magazine; September 8, 1997; p. 33
[xxx] ibid; p. 241
[xxxi] Buchanan, Lyn, *The Seventh Sense*, Paraview Pocket Books, 2003, p. 190
[xxxii] Sanction; p. 17
[xxxiii] ibid; p.17 - 18
[xxxiv] Junor; p. 20
[xxxv] Spoto; p.180
[xxxvi] Junor; p. 22
[xxxvii] *French Final Accident Report* – Conclusionary Statement section
[xxxviii] Lyall, Sarah; New York Times; December 15, 2008

Ötzi References

[xxxix] Stern, Philip Van Doren; *Prehistoric Europe - From Stone Age Man to the Early Greeks*; W.W. Norton & Company, Inc. 1969; p. 258

[xl] Ibid, p. 74

[xli] William A. Murphy, Jr, MD, Dieter zur Nedden, MD, Paul Gostner, MD, Rudolf Knapp, MD, Wolf gang Recheis PhD, and Horst Seidler, PhD; *The Iceman Discovery and Imaging* by; From the *Division of Diagnostic Imaging, University of Texas M.D. Anderson Cancer Center, Houston, TX 77030 (W.A.M.); Department of Radiology II, University of Innsbruck, Austria (D.z.N., W.R.); Department of Radiology, Regional General Hospital, Bolzano, Italy (P.G.); Department of Radiology, Kufstein Hospital, Kufstein, Austria (R.K.); and Institute for Human Biology, University of Vienna, Austria (H.S.). From the 1994 RSNA scientific assembly, published to the Internet and hereafter referred to as Abstract.*

[xlii] Baltimore SUN JOURNAL, By Michael Stroh, SUN STAFF; October 31, 2003

[xliii] Spindler, Konrad; *The Man in the Ice*; University of Innsbruck, Austria, 1993 translated by Ewald Osers; Harmony Books, 1994; p.189

[xliv] Rollo, F.U /L. Ermini/S. Luciani/, I. Marota, C. Olivieri, D. Luiselli; *The Iceman belongs to the European genetic haplogroup K and was probably infertile,* Fine characterization of the Iceman's mtDNA Haplogroup. American Journal of Physi cal Anthropology 130 (2006)

[xlv] Holzknect, Helmut, Police Officer, report on file; City of Solden, Austria.

[xlvi] *Abstract*

[xlvii] Spindler; p. 247

[xlviii] ibid; p. 182

[xlix] *Abstract*

[l] *Abstract.*

[li] *Spindler*; p. 162

[lii] *Abstract*

[liii] *Abstract*

[liv] *Spindler*; p. 182

[lv] *Abstract*

[lvi] Schöpf, Sieghart Report; Alpine Operations Group, Imst, Austria.

[lvii] McMoneagle, Joseph, *The Ultimate Time Machine*; Hampton Roads Press, 1998; p. 50

[lviii] C.B. Ruff, B.M. Holt, V. Sladek, M. Berner, W.A. Murphy jr, D. zur Nedden, H. Seidler, W. Recheis; *The Iceman's constitution was athletic, he was more a wanderer than a manual worker*; Body size, body proportions and mobility in the Tyrolean "Iceman", Journal of Human Evolution 51-1 (2006) 91-101; Seeds/ McMoneagle 1998

[lix] Loy, Tom; New Scientist Magazine article *Blood on the Axe* September 12, 1998 Center for Molecular and Cellular Biology, University of Queensland, Brisbane, Australia; p. 42 - 43

[lx] *Abstract*

[lxi] *Spindler*; p. 250

[lxii] *Spindler*; p.179

[lxiii] Jones, Tom B. *Ancient Civilization*, University of Minnesota, Rand McNally & Company, 1960 p. 15 hereafter referred to as Jones

[lxiv] Böhler, Günther; Examining Magistrate report as dictated to attorney Marelene Possik; September 23, 1991

[lxv] E-mail correspondence with Dr. Walter Leitner, Institute for Archeology, University of Innsbruck; Pre-and Early History, and Medieval Archeology and Modern Times; September 14, 2010.

[lxvi] www.de.wikipedia.org

[lxvii] www.de.Wikipedia.com; The *Langtaufers* web page

[lxviii] Ötzi's last meals: DNA analysis of the intestinal content of the Neolithic glacier mummy from the Alps; Franco Rollo, Massimo Ubaldi, Luca Ermini, and Isolina Marota, Laboratorio di Archeo-Antropologia molecolare/DNA antico, Università di Camerino, I-62032 Camerino, Italy; Edited by Francisco Mauro Salzano, Fed-deral University of Rio Grande do Sul, Porto Alegre, Brazil, and approved July 12, 2002, p. 17 - hereafter referred to as Abstract II; Seeds/McMoneagle 1998.

[lxix] *Abstract* – all three paragraphs

[lxx] http://en.wikipedia.org/wiki/%C3%96tzi

[lxxi] www.Wikipedia.com; The *Neolith* web page.

[lxxii] *Jones*; p. 16

[lxxiii] Durant, Will; *The Story of Civilization: Part I – Our Oriental Heritage*; Simon and Schuster, New York; 1954 p. 31

[lxxiv] *Durant*; p. 33

[lxxv] *Durant*; p. 34

[lxxvi] Burenhult, Goran, General Editor; *The Illustrated History of Human kind - The People of the Stone Age - Hunter-gatherers and Early Farmers*; Volume II of the Series from the American Museum of Natural History; HarperSanFrancisco; 1993, p. 106

[lxxvii] *Spindler*; p. 230

[lxxviii] *Ruff, C.B.; Biomechanical analyses of archeological human skeletons In: Katzenberg MA, Saunders SR, eds. Biological anthropology of the human skeleton. New York, NY: Wiley-Liss, 2000,*.hereafter referred to as Ruff

[lxxix] *Abstract*

[lxxx] *Abstract*

[lxxxi] www.tiscover.com

[lxxxii] Nova National Geographic Special Iceman Murder Mystery Copyright 2011, NGHT LLC., WGBH Educational Foundation

[lxxxiii] *Abstract II* - Andreas G. Heiss and Klaus Oeggl; Institute of Botany, University of Innsbruck, St,ernwartestrasse 15, 6020 Innsbruck, Austria; received: 5 December 2006 Accepted: 6 October 2007 Published online: 9 January 2008.

[lxxxiv] *Abstract II* p. 19

[lxxxv] Mauro, Salzano Francisco; Federal University of Rio Grande do Sul, Porto Alegre, Brazil, approved July 12, 2002

[lxxxvi] www.de.wikipedia.com

[lxxxvii] www.Vent.com; *A Side-Trip to South Tirol* page

[lxxxviii] *Loy*; p. 41

[lxxxix] *Abstract*

[xc] *Spindler*; p. 180

[xci] *Spindler*; p. 180

[xcii] Fowler, Brenda; *Iceman*, Random House, 2000; p.147

[xciii] *Abstract*

[xciv] *ibid*

[xcv] *ibid* – the three preceding paragraphs

[xcvi] Scientific American 79; South Tyrol Museum of Archaeology, Italy – www.sciam.com

[xcvii] *ibid*

[xcviii] Heiss, Andreas G. and Oeggl, Klaus; Institute of Botany, University of Innsbruck; published to the Internet 19, January, 2008

[xcix] *Ruff*

[c] *Abstract*

[ci] Jeanna Bryner | August 20, 2008 - http://www.livescience.com/5061-Mummified--iceman-ancient-job-determined.html

[cii] *Abstract*

[ciii] The American Heritage Dictionary of the English Language, Third Edition is

licensed from Houghton Mifflin Company. Copyright 1992
[civ] *Spindler*; p. 184
[cv] *Abstract*
[cvi] *ibid*
[cvii] *Abstract*;
[cviii] *Ruff*
[cix] Lorenzi, Rossella; *Blow to head, not arrow, killed Ötzi the Iceman*; *Discovery News*, 31 August 2007; Seeds/McMoneagle 1998
[cx] Ives, Sarah; *National Geographic News* article, October 30, 2003
[cxi] *Spindler*; p. 9
[cxii] Egarter, Gostner P, Vigl E.; *Report of radiological-forensic findings on The Ice-man. Journal of Archaeological Science 2002; 29:323-326.*
[cxiii] Dickson, Oeggl, Hanley; Scientific American, Inc. p. 79
[cxiv] Correspondence with Johanna Niederkofler; archeoParc Schnalstal/Val Senales, 2010; www.archeoparc.it
[cxv] *New radiological photos show brain trauma and prompt new theories about his death*; Lippert, A., Gostner, P., Egarter Vigl, E., Pernter, P. Vom Leben und Sterben des Ötztaler Gletschermannes. Germania 85-1 (2007) 1-21; Seeds/ McMoneagle 1998.
[cxvi] http://en.wikipedia.org/wiki/%C3%96tzi
[cxvii] Morelle, Rebecca; *Infertility link in iceman's DNA*; BBC News science reporter
[cxviii] *Spindler*; p. 189
[cxix] *Stern*; p. 288
[cxx] *Stern*; p. 226
[cxxi] Barnett, Lincoln and the Editors of *Life*; *The Epic of Man*; Golden Press, Inc. 1962; p. 37
[cxxii] *Stern*; p. 235
[cxxiii] *Jones*; p. 20
[cxxiv] Cavalli-Sforza's quote as per Wikipedia Website *Neolithic* page.
[cxxv] Price, Douglas; *Europe's First Farmers;* Cambridge University Press2000, p 5
[cxxvi] *Durant*; p. 7
[cxxvii] *Fowler*; p. 269
[cxxviii] Richburg, Keith; *Case Closed on the 'Iceman Mystery; Researchers Say Arrow Killed Bronze-Age Hunter*; The Washington Post, July 26, 2001, p. A01
[cxxix] *Richburg*; p. A01
[cxxx] Quotes from the NOVA Production by Baquared Media for WGBH Boston with ARTE France. ©2016 WGBH Educational Foundation.

Printed in Great Britain
by Amazon

40188452R00087